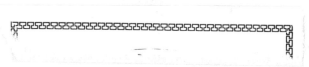

PICTORIAL HISTORY OF THE
REPUBLICAN PARTY

PICTORIAL HISTORY OF THE
REPUBLICAN PARTY

By Beryl Frank

CASTLE
BOOKS

A Division of
BOOK SALES, INC.
110 Enterprise Avenue
Secaucus, N.J. 07094

ISBN 0-89009-336-9
Library of Congress Catalog Card Number: 79-92977

Acknowledgments

The search for the pictorial history of the Republican Party began at the National Museum of History and Technology, Smithsonian Institution.

All of the photographs included here come from the files of the Smithsonian Institution.

The author wishes to acknowledge those pictures that came from the private collections of James Barnes and Kenton Broyles as well as photographs taken from the Ralph E. Becker Collection at the Smithsonian Institution.

Special thanks are offered to Mr. Herbert R. Collins, Curator, Division of Political History, Smithsonian Institution, for his assistance with this project and for writing the Special Introduction to this book.

Thanks also to the unsung heroes and heroines of the many libraries, who unfailingly answered questions of a technical nature with smiles on their faces. And most of all, thanks to Lou, who knows who he is and always understands.

Contents

Introduction

The Republican Party, as we know it today, arrived on the political scene of the United States with a jolt. Had slavery not been such a volatile issue in the 1850s, there might have been no need for a Republican Party at all.

The firecracker that started the sparks flying in all directions was the Kansas Nebraska Bill, passed by Congress on May 30, 1854. This bill allowed each of the new territories—Kansas and Nebraska—to settle the question of slavery within its own borders. It overturned the Missouri Compromise of 1850—which limited the extension of slavery—and as a result met with strong opposition from northern Democrats, Whigs, and Free Soilers.

The growth of the Republican Party from its onset in 1854 was rapid. By 1860 the young political party had accomplished its national aim—Abraham Lincoln, the presidential candidate of the party, won the national election to become the sixteenth president of the United States.

This history of the Republican Party begins with the party's appearance on the national scene. While sectional factionalism brought about the party beginnings, the party grew and changed in its concepts as the nation grew. Many Republican candidates have lived in the White House since Lincoln's time, and many other candidates have fought for the party concepts in both state and local areas. However, the story of each and every Republican would be too long a story to tell.

Primarily, this is the story of the National Republican Party—those men who sought and won the presidential elections as well as those who lost. Since 1856, the Republicans have nominated candidates for the presidency in every election. Their values, their failures, as well as their successes, are all told here in this pictorial history of the Republican Party.

Special Introduction

This book is not intended as a philosophical dissertation on the Republican Party. It presents to the readers, in pictorial fashion, a view of the origin and the machinery of the Republican Party. In a free government, the people either directly or indirectly choose their leaders by popular election. The choice is channeled through the party system. Without it, chaos would prevail. The party serves another function - that of shaping government policy and mobilizing the segments of the electorate behind such policy. It also searches out the individuals who will fill the political offices of the government and in an educational role aids in the political socialization and acculturation of a nation's people.

Our founding fathers did not ignore the existence of political parties, although provisions for such were not included in the written Constitution. Madison referred to "the spirit of party and faction" in *The Federalist* as early as 1787, and Washington referred to the "baneful effects of the spirit of the party" in his Farewell Address. Before the end of Washington's administration, rival political parties appeared on the scene. The first party was known as the Federalists, while those opposing were known simply as the Anti-Federalists. Thus, a two-party system had first been established under the new government.

From this period to the actual time of the formation of the Republican Party, the electorate and the voters who shared the ideology adopted by the Republican Party were affiliated with various parties. An attempt to collectively organize the group did not materialize until the issue of the extension of slavery divided the nation following a breakdown of the compromise policy of Clay.

The Republican Party of today had its beginnings in a little schoolhouse in Ripon, Wisconsin, in 1854. One Whig, who was in attendance, later recalled that they went in as Whigs, Free Soilers and Democrats and came out as Republicans. This meeting was soon followed by a convention in Jackson, Michigan, at which time a party platform was adopted.

In 1856, John C. Fremont became the first Presidential candidate for the newly-formed party. He was well known to the people as the young and picturesque explorer who had planted the American flag on the highest peak of the Rockies. Known as the "Pathfinder," he had the support of men like Washington Irving, Emerson, Bryant and Longfellow. His wife, who campaigned in his behalf, was the daughter of Senator Thomas Hart Benton. Despite his popularity, he lost the election.

The first major victory of the Republican Party came in 1860 with the election of Abraham Lincoln. For 68 years following that victory, the Republican Party occupied the White House with the exception of 16 years held by Democratic Presidents Cleveland and Wilson.

In his speech of February 18, 1861, Abraham Lincoln remarked: "Almost all men in this country and in any country where freedom of thought is tolerated, citizens attach themselves to political parties. It is but ordinary charity to attribute the fact that in so attaching himself to the party which his judgment prefers, the citizen believes he thereby promoted the best interest of the whole country; and when an election is passed, it is altogether befitting a free people, that until the next election, they should be as one people."

With this thought in mind, the reader of this book will more clearly understand the need for political parties in a democracy.

Herbert R. Collins

The original plans for the creation of the Republican Party were drawn up at meetings held in Ripon, Wisconsin, at the First Congregational Church on February 28, 1854 and on March 1, 1854. The Republican Party as such was born on March 20, 1854, in a schoolhouse in Ripon.

It was in this small Wisconsin schoolhouse that independent political action began—an action that united Whigs, Free Soilers, and northern Democrats in an attempt to stop the spread of slavery. The first Republican meeting at which a formal platform was adopted took place later at Jackson, Michigan, on July 6, 1854.

	Republicans	Democrats	American Know-Nothings
President:	John C. Fremont	**James Buchanan***	Millard Fillmore
Vice-President:	William L. Dayton	**John C. Breckinridge**	Andrew J. Donelson

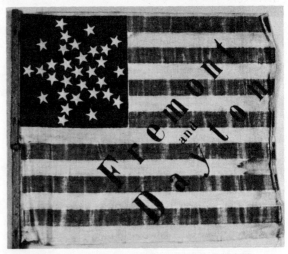

More than six hundred delegates assembled on June 17, 1856, in the city of Philadelphia at the first Republican National Convention. The delegates present included representatives from all of the free states as well as four of the border slave states. All of those who attended were united in an effort to fight slavery. The results of that convention are shown here on the flag banner. Fremont was nominated as president and William L. Dayton was to serve as his vice president.

John C. Fremont was forty-three years old when he was nominated to be president of the United States by the newly formed Republican Party. Fremont had been an army officer, an explorer known as the "pathfinder," and a senator from California. His views were definitely anti-slavery, and his nomination found favor with most of the party.

*Winning candidates will be shown in red for every election throughout the book. Only the majority losing candidates will be listed.

This banner, which tells the story of the Republican nominees as well as their platform, was made by pasting paper onto cloth. The eagle pictured here is carrying the rallying cry of "Free Soil! Free Speech! Freedom for Kansas!"

Political campaign ribbons such as this were familiar sights in the presidential election year of 1856. The play on words with free speech, free men, free territory, and Fremont was a popular cry wherever Republicans assembled.

Price 15 Cents.

THE REPUBLICAN
Campaign Songster.

COLONEL JOHN C. FREMONT.

NEW YORK AND AUBURN:
MILLER, ORTON & MULLIGAN
NEW YORK, 25 PARK ROW—AUBURN, 107 GENESEE ST.

John Fremont was popularly called "Colonel" because of his army career, and he is so named on the front of the sheet music shown here. Even though he had once been a Democrat, his strong stand against slavery and particularly against slavery in the new territories made him a popular candidate.

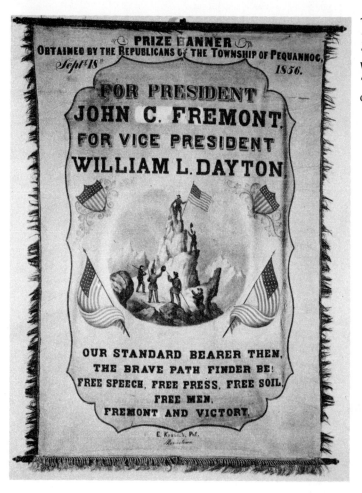

The date on this prize banner is September 18, 1856. The picture shows Fremont as the "Pathfinder" because of his exploration into the West. The Republicans hoped that the "Pathfinder" would win the presidential election, carrying them to victory in the anti-slavery fight.

This souvenir kerchief of the Know-Nothing Party stresses the idea of "Constitution and Laws." The Know-Nothings were a split from the old Whig Party and had nominated their own candidates for president and vice-president. Because they shared Republican views on the question of slavery, they served to divide the voters. It was probably this split in feelings that allowed the Democrats to win the election.

READ AND CIRCULATE.

TO CATHOLIC CITIZENS!

THE POPE'S BULL,

AND THE WORDS OF

DANIEL O'CONNELL.

NEW-YORK:
PUBLISHED BY JOSEPH H. LADD,
22 BEEKMAN STREET.

The Know-Nothing Party members, so named because they answered "I know nothing" when questioned on political issues, were also anti-Catholic in their feelings. This pamphlet, which was opposed to the extension of slavery in the United States, was issued to Catholic voters of the day.

HUNKERS, ATTEND!
FIRE AWAY!!

The above is a true likeness of "ten cent Jimmy" Buchanan, the "Damed-Black-Rat's" candidate for President.

OLD BUCK'S SONG.

Old Jimmy Buck goes in for to win,
But we go in for to beat him,
We'll hit him on the head
With a chunk of cold lead
And land him on tudder side of Jordan

FREMONT'S SONG

Ye friends of Freedom rally now
And push the cause along,
We have a glorious candidate,
A platform broad and strong.

P. S. "Jimmy" you cannot win!

Freedom's Office, FREMONT'S PEAK, Rocky Mountains.

This cartoon likens the Democratic candidate to a donkey and shows contrasting songs for both Democrat Buchanan and Republican John Fremont. The bottom line of the cartoon is an ironic postscript. Despite Republican feeling "Jimmy, you cannot win!," Buchanan did win the election to become the fifteenth president of the United States.

1860

President:
Vice-President:

Republicans	Democrats	Southern Democrats
Abraham Lincoln	Stephen A. Douglas	John C. Breckinridge
Hannibal Hamlin	Herschel V. Johnson	Joseph Lane

The Republican Convention of 1860 met in Chicago on May 16 in a specially constructed building called the Wigwam. This building was large enough to hold ten thousand cheering members of the Party, and there was a spirit of optimism emanating from the delegates and spectators alike.

The chosen candidates of the Republican Party were Illinois lawyer Abraham Lincoln for president and Senator Hannibal Hamlin of Maine for vice-president. Lincoln won the nomination on the third ballot and began the campaign that was to take him to the White House.

The Lincoln and Hamlin flag banner shown here is typical of those used at political party meetings. This one promised freedom in the territories, statehood for Kansas, and no change in the naturalization laws. The last plank was aimed at pulling in votes from the German and Irish factors in the party.

Lincoln's popularity in Illinois spread to other parts of the country during the campaign. Lithographs, like the one here by Currier and Ives made his image and that of his vice-presidential running mate well known around the country.

Senator Douglas, the stronger of the Democratic
candidates for president, believed in local control
of slavery in the territories. This, in addition to the
split in the Democratic Party, cost him many
votes.

Abe Lincoln was known as the "Rail Splitter"—a
title that indicated his modest background as a
man of the people. The cartoon shown here
portrays Lincoln riding to victory on the
Republican Party platform.

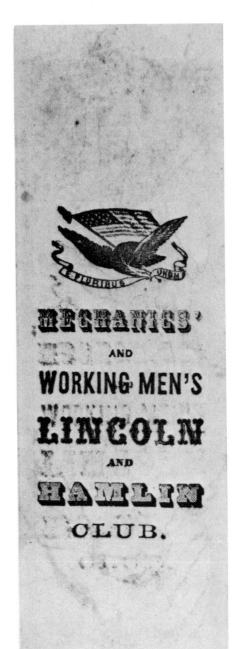

The common man did support the tall, modest Illinois lawyer as this ribbon says. Lincoln's stand on slavery, as well as his support of the Homestead law granting public land to settlers, showed his concern for that common man.

The torchlight parade became a popular method of political campaigning with parades lasting as long as three hours. The "Wide Awakes" shown here were only one political group who marched carrying banners, torches, and flags. This popular campaign technique was replaced by other methods by the beginning of the twentieth century.

This was the type of torch carried by marchers in the popular torchlight parades of the 1860s. Excitement and wild cheering went along with the torches.

The marchers in this parade were the well-drilled "Wide Awakes," and the parade for Lincoln stretched back many long blocks. It must have been an exciting sight to see the people in a parade of this length lighting up city streets with their hundreds of torches on a chilly October night in New York. It was this kind of excitement that helped win the votes needed to send Abraham Lincoln to the White House as president.

Ralph E. Becker Collection

Ralph E. Becker Collection

	Republicans	Democrats
President:	**Abraham Lincoln**	George B. McClellan
Vice-President:	**Andrew Johnson**	George H. Pendleton

Liberty and Union were major political issues for the war-torn United States. A troubled Republican Party again nominated Abraham Lincoln for the presidency at the National Convention in Baltimore. Lincoln won the nomination unanimously.

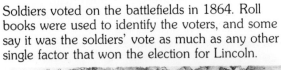

Ralph E. Becker Collection

Vice-President Hamlin was dropped at the Baltimore Republican Convention in favor of Andrew Johnson of Tennessee. Since Johnson was a southerner but a strong Union man as well, his nomination was favored by Mr. Lincoln. Johnson won the nomination for vice-president without the need for a second ballot.

Soldiers voted on the battlefields in 1864. Roll books were used to identify the voters, and some say it was the soldiers' vote as much as any other single factor that won the election for Lincoln.

This engraving from *Harper's Weekly* drawn by Thomas Nast portrays Election Day, November 8, 1864. Soldiers, veterans, and citizens were privileged to vote.

The soldiers of the Civil War were not forgotten by Republican candidate-President Abe Lincoln. The ideas "no compromise," "down with slavery," and "down with the rebels" stand out on this election-day broadside.

With Lincoln's Emancipation Proclamation in effect since January 1, 1863, these Negroes were free men entitled to the right to vote. Here they are discussing those new political rights. These voters were destined to become an important voting block to future politicians.

Democratic candidate McClellan was shown here restoring slavery to the South, while Abraham Lincoln is shown demanding that the South surrender unconditionally to the government. This was a very touchy issue throughout the country, and the final vote showed in favor of Lincoln and the Republican Party.

"YOUR PLAN AND MINE".

In 1864, the country was politically split. Some favored restoration of the Union, while others wanted total victory against the South. Jefferson Davis, as well as Democratic candidate McClellan, are shown here sinking. In the background, Abe Lincoln stands fast holding onto the Emancipation Proclamation. The Salt River, where the Democrats are headed, was a river with no ending—a political term used in the last half of the nineteenth century.

FROM OUR SPECIAL WAR CORRESPONDENT.

This cartoon by Thomas Nast appeared in *Harper's Weekly* the day that Mr. Lincoln was shot. Unlike earlier cartoons and pictures, Lincoln was pictured with his now-familiar beard.

The collection of campaign ribbons here could tell the story of President Lincoln —from the Wide Awake ribbon of his campaigns to the mourning ribbon that shows the day of his death.

Andrew Johnson became the seventeenth
president of the United States on the death of
Abraham Lincoln. It was President Johnson who
had to lead the country from war to peace and
who was the only president ever tried for
impeachment. The impeachment proceedings did
not succeed, as Johnson was acquitted by one
vote.

	Republicans	Democrats
President:	**Ulysses S. Grant**	Horatio Seymour
Vice-President:	**Schuyler Colfax**	Francis P. Blair, Jr.

Ulysses S. Grant, with his military background, was a popular man—although, he was not considered politically astute. He did, however, intend to maintain the peace of the country and for this reason won the Republican nomination for president over the very unpopular incumbent, Andrew Johnson. This sheet music refers to Lieutenant General Grant, a man the voters felt could be trusted.

Ralph E. Becker Collection

The Republican National Convention met in Chicago in May and nominated Grant for president and Schuyler Colfax, Speaker of the House from Indiana, for vice-president. Then the manufacturers got busy making campaign items. This cloth collar featuring pictures of the candidates was patented and was worn by the party faithful.

OLD COLONY & NEWPORT RAILWAY.

GRANT & COLFAX

GRAND

TORCH·LIGHT

PROCESSION IN BOSTON,

Wednesday, October 28, 1868.

FARE REDUCED!

CARS LEAVE			CARS LEAVE		
Mattapan	at	7.00 P.M.	Neponset	at	6.41 and 7.10 P.M.
Milton Lower Mills		7.03	Harrison Sq.		6.45 · 7.14
Granite Bridge		7.06	Savin Hill		6.47 · 7.17
			Crescent Ave.		6.50 · 7.20

Returning,

Will leave Boston at 12.00 P.M.

Excursion Tickets, good only to go and return on the above Extra Trains, at One Half Regular Fare.

W. H. BULLOCK, Sup't.

BOSTON, OCTOBER 24, 1868.

Torchlight parades were held in 1868 as this campaign broadside shows. While these parades generated excitement for the candidates, Mr. Grant himself was a moderate and quiet man who refused to make many speeches. Despite this, the country took him on faith in preference to the Democratic candidates of the day.

Ralph E. Becker Collection

An example of the campaign medals from each of the major parties are shown here. Seymour and Blair appear on the medal at the left, and Republican Grant is pictured on the other one.

The Republican platform was almost as moderate as the people's choice candidate. The currency plank was vague and Negro suffrage was only to be offered to the southern states, leaving the North to decide the issue by the will of its people. Rather than stressing issues, this campaign ribbon stresses the reputation of Mr. Grant as a man for peace.

VICTORY!

General Grant did overcome Seymour in the election for the presidency as this cartoon foretells. The horses being ridden by the two candidates are symbolic of their campaign. Mr. Seymour's horse is tarred on the back with the Ku Klux Klan; Grant carries a banner of Union and Equal Rights.

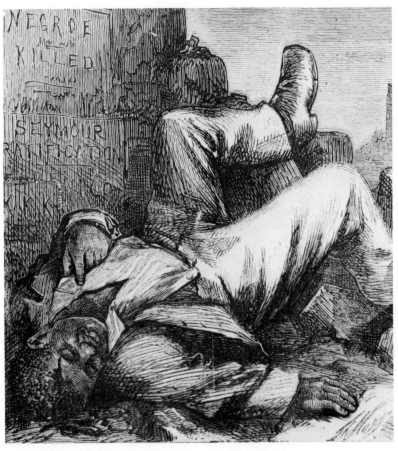

Control of the Negro vote was accomplished, according to this cartoonist, by murder. The phrases on the wall behind the dead man damn the Democrats with references to the Ku Klux Klan and the Negro killed. Although the war was over and slavery a thing of the past, the problems of post-war United States continued to center around the South. Without the Negro vote, Ulysses S. Grant might not have won the election.

UNCLE SAM'S THANKSGIVING DINNER.

Even after the election of 1868, Negro suffrage was still a political problem. Thomas Nast, noted political cartoonist for *Harper's Weekly,* featured universal suffrage and self-government in this cartoon. All races and ethnic groups were shown at the Thanksgiving table, and equality of all was the theme.

1872

President: **Ulysses S. Grant**   Horace Greeley
Vice-President: **Henry Wilson**   B. Gratz Brown

	Republicans	Democrats

There was little excitement at the Republican National Convention at Philadelphia. Grant easily won the nomination for president on his past record, and the adopted platform did not say much in the way of definitive promises. Planks were written to appeal to labor, the Negro, and even the women, but these were just pleasant generalities.

In addition to the picture of President Grant, this flag banner featured the vice-presidential nominee, Senator Henry Wilson of Massachusetts, who replaced the unpopular Schuyler Colfax.

Duxbury and Cohasset Railroad.
GRANT and WILSON
GRAND
TORCHLIGHT PROCESSION
IN BOSTON.
Wednesday Evening, Oct. 30, 1872.

EXTRA PASSENGER TRAIN.   FARES REDUCED.

CARS LEAVE		P.M.	Tickets for Round Trip.
So. Duxbury	at	5.20	$1.80
Duxbury		5.25	1.80
Webster Place		5.30	1.75
Marshfield		5.40	1.70
Marshfield Centre		5.49	1.65
Littletown		5.55	1.55
East Marshfield		6.00	1.45
So. Scituate		6.08	1.35
Scituate		6.14	1.25
Egypt		6.21	1.15
No. Scituate		6.26	1.10

RETURNING,
WILL LEAVE BOSTON AT 12.00 P.M.

Excursion Tickets good to go and return on above Extra Train may be procured at the Stations at rates specified above.

Excursion Tickets will not be sold on the train.

J. R. KENDRICK, Sup't.

BOSTON, Oct. 24, 1872.

This presidential campaign broadside features a torchlight parade in Boston. Note that round-trip fares were reduced as a special inducement to bring out-of-town people to the parade.

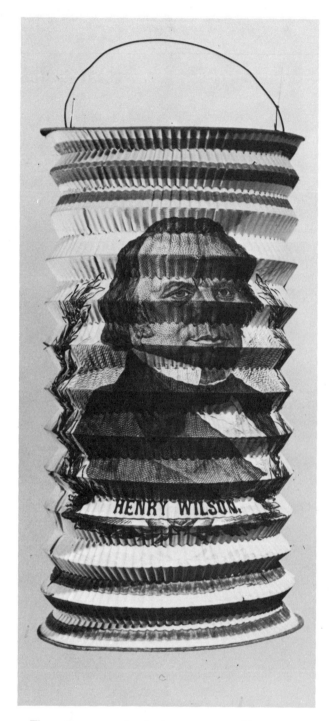

These two campaign lanterns were used in torchlight parades for the Republicans. The flag—used on the lantern for Grant and Wilson—and the candidate's picture were popular motifs.

Nine years after the peace at Appomatox, reconstruction had not as yet solved the problems of the black voter. Freed Negroes were still threatened with guns at the polls. However, the Republican Party did not underestimate the strength of their votes.

President:

Vice-President:

Republicans

Rutherford B. Hayes

William A. Wheeler

Democrats

Samuel J. Tilden

Thomas A. Hendricks

In this collection of campaign ribbons, both the Democratic and Republican candidates are shown for the year 1876. The 15th Ward, the center ribbon, urges the voter to cast a ballot for the entire Republican ticket.

The Republican National Convention met on June 14 in Cincinnati, Ohio, and nominated Ohio's governor, Rutherford B. Hayes, for the presidency. New York Congressman William A. Wheeler was named for the vice-presidency. Both men were proven vote-getters, and the campaign was underway.

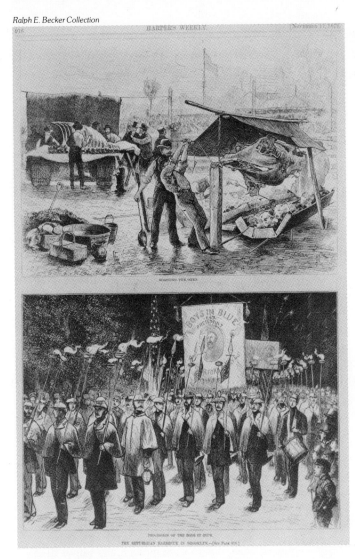

This barbecue and torchlight parade in Brooklyn, New York, was typical of the mass demonstrations used to maintain party fervor and loyalty. The participants ate together, marched together, and hopefully voted together.

The election of 1876 was one of the most hotly contested in the history of the United States. It was necessary to appoint a special Electoral Commission to decide upon the winner. The electoral count began on February 1, 1877, and was not completed until March 2. Democratic candidate Tilden had 184 votes, while Hayes won by just one vote with a count of 185. President Hayes took the oath of office on March 3.

1880

President:
Vice-President:

Republicans
James A. Garfield
Chester A. Arthur

Democrats
Winfield S. Hancock
William H. English

JAMES A. GARFIELD.

This engraving of James A. Garfield shows the candidate as a youth who was born in a log cabin, as a soldier who served in the Civil War, and as a statesman, the senator-elect from Ohio. The young man, only forty-eight years old when nominated for the presidency, was well received by the Republican Party.

Nominations by the National Republican Party for the candidates in 1880 took place in Chicago at the Exposition Building shown here. Garfield, in his capacity as Chairman of the Rules Committee, passed a rule that may have won him the nomination. This rule recognized the rights of delegates to vote individually rather than as a state unit.

Politically, one of the most powerful pens in the country was that of Thomas Nast, cartoonist for *Harper's Weekly*. Nast is credited with giving both major political parties their animal symbols. His use of the elephant for the Republicans and the donkey for the Democrats caught on in 1880 and is still going strong.

"THE COMING CROWN."
A Republican victory, and an everlasting Republican form of government.

Thomas Nast drew this cartoon for the May 15, 1880, issue of *Harper's Weekly*. The cartoon showed Nast's faith in the power of the people, when they exercised their right to vote. The ballot box shown here is more than a privilege—it is a responsibility.

Since President Hayes held fast to his belief in a one-term presidency, the way was open for Garfield and his running mate, Chester A. Arthur of New York. The campaign bandanna shows both of the Republican candidates for the country's highest offices.

After the exceptionally honest administration of President Hayes, the Democrats could not do much mudslinging on the Republican record in the White House. The contest presented to the voters was almost a popularity contest, with Garfield being the most popular. This Grand National Banner shows both candidates as clean, honorable men with the eagle and the flag standing behind them.

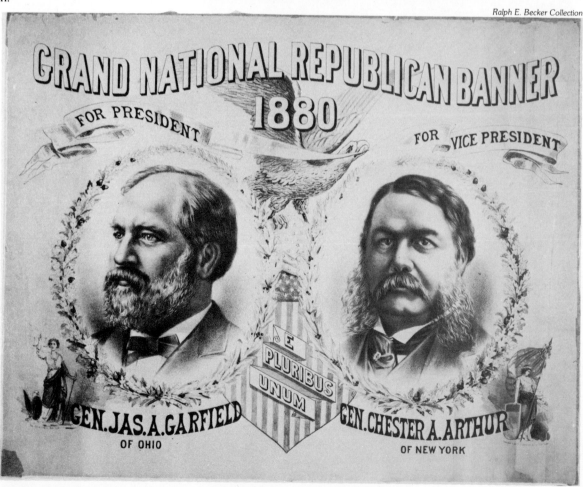

Campaign plates were popular in the campaign of 1880, and this one bearing Garfield's picture was typical of the kind available at that time.

This textile showing Garfield's picture was printed in 1880 for Garfield's campaign for the presidency. The quilt-like design of the textile was typical of the patchwork quilting done in many American homes at that time.

Elegant, sophisticated Chester A. Arthur of New York was sworn into office as president on September 20, 1881, after the death of Garfield. His urbanity and good looks endeared him to the country, although he only served out the remainder of his term and was not reelected to office.

The July after his inauguration, Garfield was wounded by an assassin's bullet. Three months later, on September 19, 1881, he died as a result of those wounds. It is not known whether Garfield would have been a significant president, but his untimely death saddened the entire country. Sheet music such as this funeral march was widely circulated at that time.

	Republicans	Democrats
President:	James G. Blaine	**Grover Cleveland**
Vice-President:	John A. Logan	**Thomas A. Hendricks**

Ralph E. Becker Collection

The Republican Party convened in Chicago for their national convention on June 3. This cover of *Harper's Weekly* shows the torchlight parade that took place during the convention. Flags and torches were held high to create enthusiasm for the candidates.

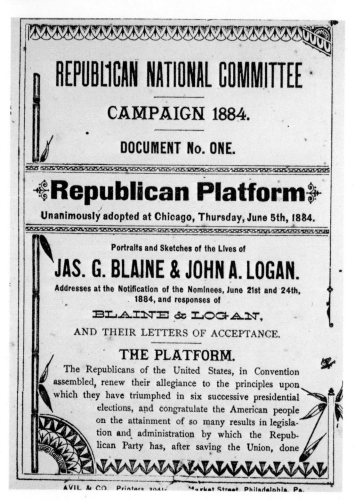

The party platform that was adopted in Chicago was rather vague on major issues. It stressed the idea that the Republicans had saved the Union and repeated vague pledges made in earlier platforms. It was not the issues that were to win the election, but rather the candidates themselves.

The Republican candidate for president was the Honorable James G. Blaine, congressman from Maine. His running mate was Senator John A. Logan of Illinois. Both men had been prominent in politics for many years.

As a result of both party conventions, the two main candidates for president in 1884 were James G. Blaine for the Republicans and Grover Cleveland of New York for the Democrats. The campaign was to be an ugly contest with mudslinging from both sides.

"The best 5 ct. SEGARS in the country" were CAPADURAS, and the company was advertising for the Republican Party. Logan is offering the SEGARS to "the Boys" as a means of gaining their votes. Tobacco advertising as a method of promoting the candidate was quite prevalent in 1884.

LOGAN—We've got the nomination, but to get elected we must keep the Boys supplied with
·CAPADURAS·
The best 5 CT. SEGARS in the country.
BLAINE — Right you are, GENERAL!

Compliments of
DOYLE & SMITH,
Cigar Makers,
ONEONTA, N. Y.

The effects of a Tariff exclusively for Revenue as laid down in the Democratic Platform and which the Democratic Congressmen tried to enact last winter at Washington.

Democratic Free-Trade Means low wages, children in rags and ignorance

If you are satisfied with this picture vote for Cleveland and Hendricks.

And P. V. DEUSTER the Free Trader.

The effects of Protection to American Industries as guaranteed by the Republican Party and Platform.

Republican Protection Means good wages, happy homes and education for your children

If you prefer this picture vote for Blaine and Logan.

And ISAAC W. VAN SCHAI

Protection for American industries was shown in this cartoon to be a prime party plank for the Republicans. "Good wages, happy homes, and education for your children" were all promised by the cartoonist if the Republicans were to win the election.

JAMES G. BLAINE
OF MAINE

JOHN A. LOGAN
OF ILLINOIS

This bandanna, showing pictures of both Republican candidates, was a popular campaign item of the day.

48

We may differ in Politics   but We all agree that.

HOW BLAINE GREW RICH IN OFFICE.

BLAINE'S HOUSE IN AUGUSTA, 1862.

BLAINE'S MANSION IN WASHINGTON.
(See the Other Side.)

Although prohibition was not a major issue yet, the Prohibitionists were definitely at work in 1884. However, according to this cartoon, neither of the major candidates were in favor of prohibition, as they were both shown imbibing at the same table. Cleveland sits to the left of the waiter and Blaine sits to the right.

Blaine was accused by the Democrats of growing wealthy during his time in office. This was due to his involvement in a railroad deal that was considered quite shady. Blaine had to defend his honor in 1876, and the scandal haunted him again in 1884. In addition to the charges of bribery and double dealing, Blaine had an Irish Catholic mother, which was brought into the campaign as well.

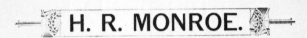

MA, MA, Where's My Pa

UP IN THE

White House, Dear!

—BY—

H. R. MONROE.

Published By
National Music Company Chicago
215 to 221 Wabash Ave

The Republicans did their share of ugly mudslinging when they accused Grover Cleveland of fathering an illegitimate child. Although the accusation was never proven to be true, the song *Ma, Ma, Where's My Pa* was loudly chorused by the Republican opposition.

The train pulling into the station of Augusta, Maine, was typical of the type of campaigning done in 1884. The train was decorated with signs, and the flag flew proudly for Blaine.

Ralph E. Becker Collection

The political discussion taking place here in a country store questions whether Mr. Blaine should win the election when he "so shamefully lowered the moral tone of the Party?" Conservative and progressive Republicans debated this question all over the country.

Satire appeared frequently in *Judge* cartoons, and the satire here was directed at the Woman's Rights Movement and Belva Lockwood, the movement's candidate. The prohibition issue was shown here as the way to "Ruin the Republican Party."

Each of these political playing cards featured a candidate or issue of the day. The King of Hearts is Grover Cleveland. The Queen resembles Blaine. The Jack of Spades talks of the fraud of 1876, while the Queen of Clubs shows the unfulfilled promises of the Democrats for forty acres and a mule. Cards like these are collector's items today but were common in the campaign of 1884.

	Republicans	Democrats
President:	**Benjamin Harrison**	Grover Cleveland
Vice-President:	**Levi P. Morton**	Allen G. Thurman

Respectfully Dedicated to the Hon. Ben. Harrison "Tippecanoe & Morton Too".

HARRISON'S VICTORY MARCH

FOR PIANO OR CABINET ORGAN.
Composed by CLIFFORD HALE.

Senator Benjamin Harrison of Indiana won the presidential nomination at the Republican National Convention in Chicago in June. Born in Ohio, but by then a resident of the Hoosier State, Harrison brought with him the support of Indiana. As the grandson of William Henry Harrison, and a man who had served well in the Civil War, Harrison was the chosen man to lead the Republicans. The sheet music shown here refers to the old campaign cry of William Henry Harrison with a new twist, as it cheers "Tippecanoe and Morton, too."

The vice-presidential candidate was Levi P. Morton, a banker and businessman from New York. Since Indiana and New York were both key states in the election of 1888, the choice of Morton complemented the choice of Harrison. Politically, the bandanna shown here asserts that both Harrison and Morton will protect the home industry—a major issue in the campaign.

Both Republican and Democratic headquarters in New York City were decorated with banners of their candidates. Once again, Harrison and Morton were pledged to protect home industries, while the Democrats were planning to reduce tariffs.

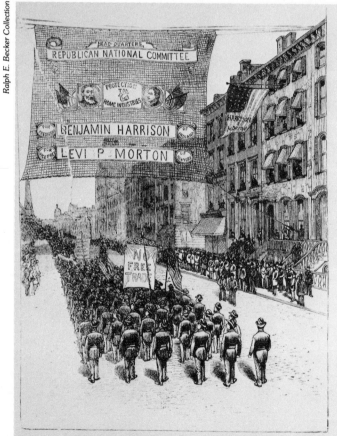

THE REPUBLICAN HEADQUARTERS, 91 FIFTH AVENUE.

THE DEMOCRATIC HEADQUARTERS, TWENTY-NINTH STREET, NEAR BROADWAY.

THE PRESIDENTIAL CAMPAIGN-HEADQUARTERS OF THE REPUBLICAN AND DEMOCRATIC NATIONAL COMMITTEES, IN NEW YORK CITY.

The Republican songs of the day reflected the idea that the people did not want to reelect Grover Cleveland. In this campaign, there was less mudslinging than there was in the campaign of 1884. It was Cleveland's policies, rather than his personal life, that were criticized.

Here, Harrison and Morton—and the Republican Party as well—are shown with the sword of Cleveland's popularity hanging over their heads. Note the issues of prohibition and tariff decorating the cake at the right side of the table.

WORKINGMEN!

WHICH DO YOU WANT?
AMERICAN OR EUROPEAN WAGES!

POTTERIES.

	English	Trenton, N. J.
Plate makers,	$7 75	$20 40
Dish makers,	9 67	19 43
Cup makers,	9 97	18 50
Saucer makers,	7 97	18 50
Wash bowl makers,	9 71	25 64
Pressers,	8 18	17 12
Printers,	6 59	13 56
Kilnmen,	6 59	12 00
Saggar makers,	8 50	17 00
Mould makers,	10 29	20 00
Turners,	8 05	18 00
Handlers,	8 43	19 00

WINDOW GLASS.

	Ohio Valley Average, per Week	Belgium Average, per W'k
Blowers,	$40 09	$20 00
Gatherers,	23 03	6 25
Flatners,	34 45	6 25
Cutters,	27 59	5 00

COAL MINERS AND COKE MAKERS.
TIME, TEN HOURS PER DAY.

Occupation.	W. Va. Wages, per Day.	English Wages, per Day
Blacksmiths,	$2 00	$1 14
Blacksmiths' helpers,	1 25	72
Coal cleaner,	1 25	60
Drivers,	1 60	50
Engineers,	1 75	1 12
Furnacemen,	1 25	72
Laborers,	1 25	72
Miners,	1 40 to 1 87	1 12
Mine boss,	2 50	1 68
Track layer,	1 80	90
Trappers,	50	22
Weighers,	1 80	90

BLAST FURNACES.

	Ohio Valley per Day.	Cumberland, Eng., per Day
Keepers,	$2 25	$1 41
Helpers,	1 65	85
Top fillers,	1 65	1 13
Bottom fillers,	1 65	1 13
Cinder loaders,	1 55	85
Blast engineer,	2 25	1 00
Cindermen,	1 65	1 11
General labor,	1 40	77

The wages of Blast Furnaces here denominated as Ohio Valley wages are the smallest west of the Allegheny Mountains. Those paid in Joliet, Ill., and even in Pittsburgh, are higher than those given here.

ROLLING MILL.

	West of Allegheny M'tn's, per Ton.	England, per Ton.
Puddling,	$5 50	$1 57
Muck rolling,	68¼	24
Bar rolling and catching,	1 13¾	73
Bar heating,	70	34
Hoop rolling and heating 1½" and No. 17,	3 50	1 80
Cotton tie rolling and heating,	4 10	2 37

BESSEMER STEEL WORKS.

	United States, per Day.	England, per Day
Converter men,	$4 35, 12 h'rs.	$1 45
Steel works pit men,	4 00, 8 "	1 15 to 1 25
Steel works ladle men,	3 98, 12 "	1 00 to 1 15
Rail heaters,	5 00, 12 "	1 60
Rail rollers,	7 00, 12 "	2 50
Common laborers,	1 34, 10 "	62
(June, 1888.)		

FLINT GLASS WORKERS.

	WEST VIRGINIA WAGES, PER DAY.	GREAT BRITAIN WAGES, PER DAY
Glass blowers, Pressers and Finishers,	$3 25 to 4 25	$ 96 to 1 20
First-class Castor place Workmen,	4 50 to 6 00	1 25 to 2 40
Punch Tumbler Blowers,	1 50 to 3 75	65 to 96

The hours of work in Europe are longer than in America for the same amount of work.

According to this poster, American workers were earning more than their counterparts in Europe. If the Republicans could win the election, they promised to continue tariff policies that would insure the higher wages and lower working hours.

Campaign Eggs Given Away

TO ALL PURCHASERS OF
CLOTHING.

I CROW FOR

Cleveland
—OR—
Harrison.

The Greatest Campaign Novelty Out.
—CALL AT—

MYERS & HEIM, 508 Penn St.

Billed as the greatest campaign novelty, the egg shown here with the candidate of the voter's choice on it was presented free to any purchasers of clothing at this store. The ad appeared in the *Daily Times and Dispatch* of Reading, Pennsylvania, on November 8, 1888.

The irony of this anti-Democratic cartoon was the weak tightrope on which Cleveland was balanced. The small print at the bottom of the cartoon reads, "Cleveland will have a walk-over—so the Democratic Newspapers say."

Protection for the American workingman was featured in this *Judge* cartoon. Free trade with England would have hurt labor in this country; for this reason, Harrison and the Republicans were opposed to tariff reduction.

DEMOCRATIC
National Ticket.

For President
Grover Cleveland,
Of New York.

For Vice-President
Allen G. Thurman,
Of Ohio.

FOR PRESIDENTIAL ELECTORS,
Electors-at-Large.
William D. Hill,

William W. Ellsberry.

District Electors.
John E. Bell,

James D. Parker,

Henry Miller,

Frederick B. Kampf,

Albert M. Ensminger,

Frederick W. LeSueur,

Harry C. Armstrong,

Samuel W. Courtright,

Daniel Flanagan,

George C. Beis,

Irvine Dungan,

Thomas W. Higgins,

William P. Price,

David S. Sampsell, Sr.,

Daniel B. Torpy,

Herman F. Achauer,

William H. Hunter,

Anthony Howells,

Daniel B. Woods,

John J. Hall,

Augustus Zehring.

Democratic State Ticket.
For Secretary of State.
BOSTON G. YOUNG.

For Judge of the Supreme Court.
LYMAN R. CRITCHFIELD.

For Member of the Board of Public Works.
JAMES EMMITT.

Democratic Congressional Ticket.
For Representative to Congress for the
9th Congressional District.
JOHN S. BRADDOCK.

Democratic Judicial Ticket.
For Judge of the Circuit Court of the
5th Judicial Circuit.
CHARLES FOLLETT.

Democratic County Ticket.
For Sheriff.
WILBERT MAIN.

For Prosecuting Attorney.
FRANK M. MARRIOTT.

For Commissioner.
JOHN W. CULVER.

For Infirmary Director.
RANSOM CAMPBELL.

For Coroner.
R. C. RITCHIE.

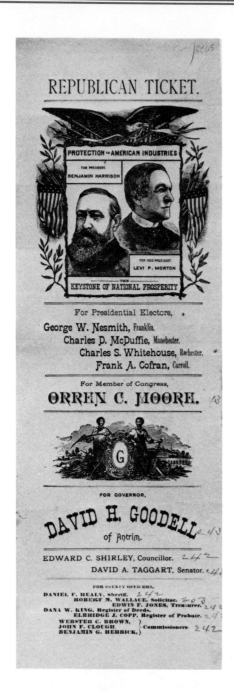

REPUBLICAN TICKET.

PROTECTION TO AMERICAN INDUSTRIES
FOR PRESIDENT
BENJAMIN HARRISON

FOR VICE PRESIDENT
LEVI P. MORTON

THE
KEYSTONE OF NATIONAL PROSPERITY

For Presidential Electors,
George W. Nesmith, Franklin.
Charles P. McDuffie, Manchester.
Charles S. Whitehouse, Rochester.
Frank A. Cofran, Carroll.

For Member of Congress,
ORREN C. MOORE.

FOR GOVERNOR,
DAVID H. GOODELL
of Antrim.

EDWARD C. SHIRLEY, Councillor.

DAVID A. TAGGART, Senator.

FOR COUNTY OFFICERS.
DANIEL F. HEALY, Sheriff.
ROBERT M. WALLACE, Solicitor.
EDWIN F. JONES, Treasurer.
DANA W. KING, Register of Deeds.
ELBRIDGE J. COPP, Register of Probate.
WEBSTER C. BROWN,
JOHN F. CLOUGH, } Commissioners.
BENJAMIN G. HERRICK,

1888.

This is the Regular and only Genuine
REPUBLICAN TICKET.
H. S. Gere, Chairman Co. Com.

FOR PRESIDENT,
BENJAMIN HARRISON. of Indiana.

FOR VICE-PRESIDENT,
LEVI P. MORTON. - of New York.

FOR PRESIDENTIAL ELECTORS—AT LARGE.
GEORGE D. ROBINSON,   WILLIAM F. DRAPER,
OF CHICOPEE.   OF HOPEDALE.
BY DISTRICTS.
1.—JOHN H. REED, - - of Barnstable.
2.—GEORGE E. FREEMAN, - of Brockton.
3.—HALSEY J. BOARDMAN, - of Boston.
4.—ELIJAH MERTAIN HATCH, - of Boston.
5.—HENRY J. WELLS, - - of Cambridge.
6.—HORATIO WELLINGTON, - of Boston.
7.—FRANCIS NORWOOD, - of Beverly.
8.—CHARLES U. BELL, - of Lawrence.
9.—CHARLES Q. TIRRELL, - of Natick.
10.—FRANK P. GOULDING, - - of Worcester.
11.—CHESTER C. CONANT, - of Greenfield.
12.—ELISHA MORGAN, - of Springfield.

FOR GOVERNOR,
OLIVER AMES, - - - of Easton.
FOR LIEUTENANT-GOVERNOR,
JOHN Q. A. BRACKETT. - of Arlington.
FOR SECRETARY OF THE COMMONWEALTH,
HENRY B. PEIRCE, - of Abington.
FOR TREASURER AND RECEIVER-GENERAL,
GEORGE A. MARDEN, - - of Lowell.
FOR AUDITOR,
CHARLES R. LADD. - - of Springfield.
FOR ATTORNEY-GENERAL,
ANDREW J. WATERMAN. - of Pittsfield.
FOR REPRESENTATIVE TO CONGRESS—Eleventh District,
RODNEY WALLACE, - of Fitchburg.
FOR COUNCILLOR—Eighth District,
LEVI J. GUNN. - - of Greenfield.
FOR SENATOR—Berkshire and Hampshire District,
ALFRED S. FASSETT, of Great Barrington.
FOR COUNTY COMMISSIONER—Hampshire County,
ELISHA A. EDWARDS, - of Southampton.
FOR REGISTER OF DEEDS—Hampshire County,
HENRY P. BILLINGS, - of Northampton.
FOR REGISTER OF PROBATE AND INSOLVENCY—Hampshire County,
HUBBARD M. ABBOTT, - of Northampton.
FOR COUNTY TREASURER—Hampshire County,
LEWIS WARNER, - of Northampton.
FOR REPRESENTATIVES—First Hampshire District,
JOHN B. BOTTUM, - of Northampton.
GEORGE K. EDWARDS, - of Southampton.

Ralph E. Becker Collection

The idea of protection for American industries
was carried out and stressed on the Republican
tickets. This was considered the keystone of
national prosperity.

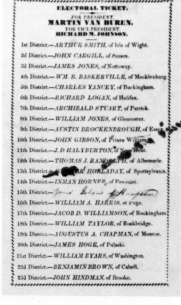

ELECTORAL TICKET.
FOR PRESIDENT
MARTIN VAN BUREN.
FOR VICE PRESIDENT
RICHARD M. JOHNSON.

1st District.—ARTHUR SMITH, of Isle of Wight.
2d District.—JOHN CARGILL, of Sussex.
3d District.—JAMES JONES, of Nottoway.
4th District.—WM. R. BASKERVILLE, of Mecklenburg.
5th District.—CHARLES YANCEY, of Buckingham.
6th District.—RICHARD LOGAN, of Halifax.
7th District.—ARCHIBALD STUART, of Patrick.
8th District.—WILLIAM JONES, of Gloucester.
9th District.—AUSTIN BROCKENBROUGH, of Essex.
10th District.—JOHN GIBSON, of Prince William.
11th District.—J. D. HALYBURTON, of New Kent.
12th District.—THOMAS J. RANDOLPH, of Albemarle.
13th District.— HOLLADAY, of Spottsylvania.
14th District.—INMAN HORNER, of Fauquier.
15th District.— of Hampton.
16th District.—WILLIAM A. HARRIS, of Page.
17th District.—JACOB D. WILLIAMSON, of Rockingham.
18th District.—WILLIAM TAYLOR, of Rockbridge.
19th District.—AUGUSTUS A. CHAPMAN, of Monroe.
20th District.—JAMES HOGE, of Pulaski.
21st District.—WILLIAM BYARS, of Washington.
22d District.—BENJAMIN BROWN, of Cabell.
23d District.—JOHN HINDMAN, of Brooke.

Woman's Suffrage was an issue that was gaining momentum in 1888. The leaders of the 1888 Suffrage Convention are shown here with Susan B. Anthony in the center. The women were demanding the right to vote from both major parties. Their intention to participate in the democratic process was not considered a serious problem by the men of the day, although the women had been organized since 1848.

A suffrage convention was held in Washington, D.C., in 1888. Although the women were conservatively dressed, they were considered very forward, as this was a politically unpopular issue at the time. Republicans, as well as Democrats, considered this an unimportant issue.

Many pictures of this time do not show women at the polls, but the women were working hard. This wood engraving after a photograph by Kirkland appeared in *Frank Leslie's Illustrated Newspaper* on November 24, 1888. Although Wyoming was still just a territory, the women were out to get the vote.

These tickets were put out by the Republican Party to send the Democrats up the proverbial Salt River to oblivion. They apparently were a successful campaign gimmick and did contribute to the Republicans taking the election in the year of 1888.

	Republicans	Democrats
President:	Benjamin Harrison	Grover Cleveland
Vice-President:	Whitelaw Reid	Adlai E. Stevenson

Beaver hats were in vogue for the gentlemen of 1892, and inside the hat shown here were the two Republican candidates, Benjamin Harrison and Whitelaw Reid. As in the campaign of 1888, protection of home industry was an important issue.

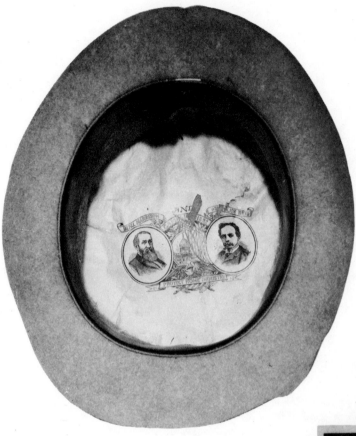

Ralph E. Becker Collection

This paper napkin showing pictures of the Republican candidates may have been used at the Republican National Convention. Harrison was nominated to succeed himself as president, and Reid of New York was his running mate.

Tobacco advertising was a still-popular way of keeping the candidates names before the public. The man who bought these cigars was probably an ardent Republican.

The National Republican Convention began on June 7, 1892, in Minneapolis. The choice of this site for the convention was an attempt to gather more support for the party from this part of the country. The platform adopted here offered nothing new, as it was a continuation of Republican policies during Harrison's term of office.

This collection of presidential campaign ribbons featured the incumbent, President Harrison. His picture, as well as his constant cry of protection for the American worker, appeared frequently in campaign material.

As in many earlier campaign bandannas, the flag colors, as well as pictures of the Republican candidates, were featured.

Torchlight parades were still popular for political candidates. These portraits of Harrison and Reid were carried by a faithful party follower in 1892.

Although the issue of prohibition was not featured by the Republicans at this time, this cartoon indicates that President Harrison was opposed to whiskey. He is shown first enjoying a soda with the ladies and then pointing a negative finger at the bartender.

	Republicans	Democrats
President:	**William McKinley**	William Jennings Bryan
Vice-President:	**Garret A. Hobart**	Arthur Sewall

After the panic of 1893 and the depression that followed it, it was only natural that the Republicans blamed the Democrats for the problems of the country. The cloth banner, which pictures the Republican candidates for president and vice-president, stresses financial stability as a mark of the Republican Party. Clean-shaven, honest Governor William McKinley of Ohio was the party's choice.

McKinley's headquarters in Chicago during this campaign were in the Auditorium building. The women pictured here were probably secretaries and typists.

Black workers were prominent in the Chicago campaign office for McKinley in 1896. Their vote was important to Mr. McKinley, since he needed the support of the South to win the election.

Such personal items as a comb and brush set were used as campaign material for McKinley. The slogan, "A Clean Sweep," promised Republican prosperity as opposed to Democratic depression.

A glass serving dish with its picture of the Republican candidate for president found its way into many Republican homes. "Protection and plenty" were to be found with a vote for McKinley.

The top of this pin cushion reads, "Pin your faith to honest money." Although McKinley's campaign was managed by "Boss" Marcus Hanna, a veteran politician, the country at large felt that McKinley was definitely an honest man.

Governor McKinley of Ohio was a tactful and cautious man, skilled in the art of compromise. He had a formal friendliness and good appearance, as shown on this match case, and despite his political ties with Mark Hanna was very much his own man.

The gold bugs shown on the original sales display board here reflected McKinley's position on the currency issue. He favored the moderate gold plank in the party platform, although he had once been sympathetic toward free silver.

This cartoon appeared in *Wasp* and supported the gold standard for currency by showing all the evils of free silver throughout the world. Democratic candidate Bryan was strongly in favor of free silver, causing this to be one of the most vocal issues in the campaign of 1896.

BALLEWS

GOLD BUG.

REPUBLICAN.

FROM WASP.

DEMOCRATIC CAMPAIGN HEADQUARTERS.

VOTE FOR FREE SILVER & BE PROSPEROUS LIKE GUATEMALA

VOTE FOR FREE SILVER & BE PROSPEROUS LIKE INDIA 2¢ A DAY

VOTE FOR FREE SILVER & BE PROSPEROUS LIKE SOUTH AMERICA 20¢ A DAY

VOTE FOR FREE SILVER & BE PROSPEROUS LIKE JAPAN 15¢ A DAY

VOTE FOR FREE SILVER & BE PROSPEROUS LIKE CHINA 10¢ A DAY

VOTE FOR FREE SILVER & BE PROSPEROUS LIKE MEXICO 25¢ A DAY

DUBIOUS.

"What awful poor wages they get in all those free silver countries, John!"
"That's so, wife, but the politicians say it will be different in America."
"I wouldn't take any chances on it, John. It's easy to lower wages and hard to raise them. Politicians will tell you anything. We know there was good wages when we had protection. We could never buy clothes for the children on what they get in those free silver countries, could we?"

Republican political umbrellas featured the pictures of both candidates as well as the slogans for Protection and Sound Money.

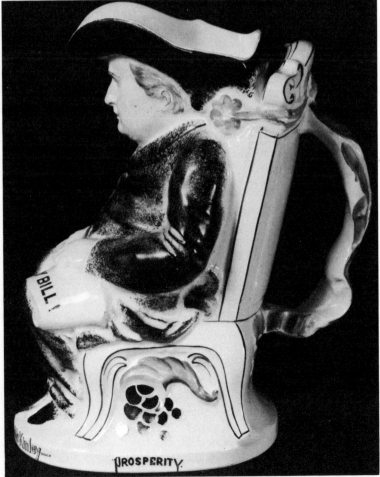

Toby jugs bearing McKinley slogans were popular in the campaign of 1896. Finding such a piece of political memorabilia today would be a collector's delight.

Governor McKinley was a devoted husband to his invalid wife and remained with her in their home in Canton, Ohio, as much as possible. Obviously, from the look on her face in this picture and the campaign ribbon she wears, she was behind her husband all the way.

Since McKinley would not go to the people, he invited the people to come to him. Here he is shown speaking to a crowd from the front porch of his own home in Canton, Ohio. Because of the many speeches he gave here, his campaign became known as the "Front Porch Campaign." Although these tactics were unusual in 1896, they did manage to win him election to the highest office in the United States.

	Republicans	Democrats
President:	**William McKinley**	William Jennings Bryan
Vice-President:	**Theodore Roosevelt**	Adlai E. Stevenson

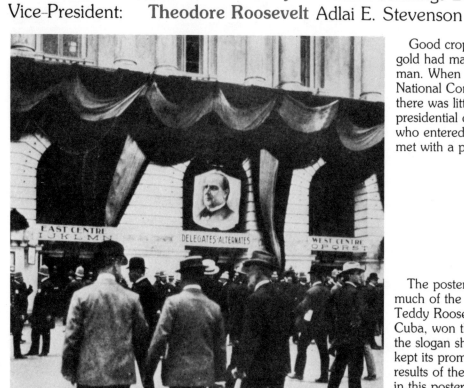

Good crops, rising prices, and new sources of gold had made President McKinley a popular man. When the Republicans met for their National Convention in Philadelphia in June, there was little question that he would be their presidential candidate. The Republican voters who entered the hall to cast their ballots were met with a picture of McKinley overhead.

The poster contrasting 1896 with 1900 tells much of the story of the Republicans of 1900. Teddy Roosevelt, the hero of San Juan Hill in Cuba, won the nomination for vice-president, and the slogan showing that the administration had kept its promises was a popular theme. Even the results of the Spanish-American War were shown in this poster—Americans were shown teaching Cuban children in contrast to the prisons of Spanish rule.

As stated here the "Real Issue" was opposition to free silver. The paper Mr. McKinley holds in his hand reads as follows: "I do not know what you think about it, but I believe it is a good deal better to open up the mills of the United States to the labor of America than to open up the mints of the United States to the silver of the World."

Political buttons were sold in large quantities. If the men looking at the buttons for sale in 1900 were Republicans, they undoubtedly chose one bearing a likeness to President McKinley.

Pictures of both of the Republican candidates were imposed on the flag. Prosperity at home and prestige abroad were to become bywords of the national campaign.

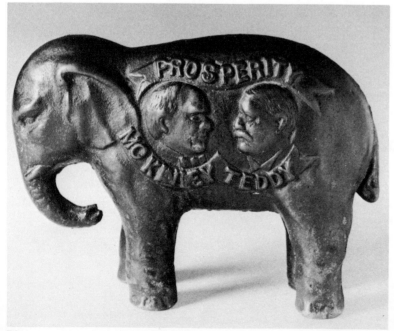

This cast-iron elephant bank bears the name of McKinley and "Teddy." Although the "Rough Rider," who had taken San Juan Hill during the Spanish-American War, did not particularly care for the nickname, the people did. Teddy was a rough diamond who was readily accepted by the country at large.

Pictures of Mr. McKinley and Teddy Roosevelt were included as part of the design of this handsome pocket watch. Pocket watches were in vogue at the time, and this one must have been carried by an ardent Republican.

Although McKinley was known for his "Front Porch Campaign," he also made speeches on his own behalf. Here he is shown in San Jose, California, with Mrs. McKinley seated behind him.

The full dinner pail in this *Judge* cartoon was a symbol of the humble prosperity to which McKinley said he owed his reelection. The feeling among Republicans was that the gold standard would continue that prosperity.

In 1900, cartoons were drawn by those against prohibition as well as those in favor of it. This anti-prohibition cartoon states, "The only solution of the liquor problem—wise and fair restrictions." There were people in both parties at this time who were against the temperance movement, but the Prohibitionists continued to make themselves heard.

This collection of First Lady campaign buttons, which comes from three different campaigns, shows that the country wanted to know the wives of their candidates. Grover Cleveland is shown with Mrs. Frances Cleveland on one of the buttons. The 1896 button pictures Mrs. McKinley and the third button, a funeral button, shows both of the McKinleys and their home in Canton, Ohio. The small print on that reads, "It is God's way. His will be done. Not Ours."

Although McKinley was reelected to office, he did not live to complete his term. Shot on September 6, 1901, he died on September 19. Teddy Roosevelt was vacationing in the Adirondacks when he heard the news of the fatal bullet. As a result of that bullet, he became the twenty-sixth president of the United States.

1904

President:
Vice-President:

Republicans
Theodore Roosevelt
Charles W. Fairbanks

Democrats
Alton B. Parker
Henry G. Davis

Ralph E. Becker Collection

There was little question that the Republican National Convention in Chicago would nominate Teddy Roosevelt for president. Both he and his running mate, Senator Charles W. Fairbanks of Indiana, won by acclamation.

The Republican candidates upheld the Party platform, which promised liberty, protection, and prosperity. They intended to keep these promises by upholding the protective tariff system and preserving the gold standard.

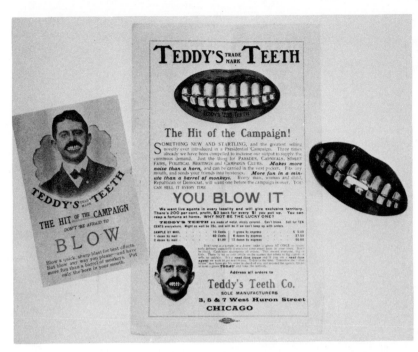

Teddy's Teeth were a popular campaign novelty in the campaign of 1904. The small print of the advertisement reads, "Every man, woman and child, Republican or Democrat, will want one before the campaign is over."

This well-circulated picture of President Roosevelt entertaining Booker T. Washington at the White House became the object of a particularly ugly type of political mudslinging—it was used to promote views both against and in favor of the racial issue, depending on where it was used. In the North, the picture made Washington look caucasian, while in the South Washington was made to look more African. This picture, with Lincoln in the background, was also used on political campaign buttons of the day.

DINNER GIVEN AT THE WHITE HOUSE BY PRESIDENT ROOSEVELT TO BOOKER T. WASHINGTON, OCTOBER 17th, 1901

The pictures around the border of this Republican bandanna show the positive side of Republican policies of protection, expansion, prosperity, and sound money.

The Gold Bug is only one of the popular Republican Party pins used in 1904. Other novelties were T.R.'s eyeglasses, the Teddy Bear pin, as well as the more usual type of picture buttons.

This meerschaum pipe was a usable political novelty in 1904. The gentleman who smoked could campaign for his candidate with a pipe bearing the head of Roosevelt.

President Roosevelt was campaigning in top hat with Senator George F. Hoar of Massachusetts in an open horse and carriage. When the people saw Teddy, they loved him.

Roosevelt was an ecologist before people knew the word. He was always interested in preserving the natural resources of our country. Here he is shown on horseback at Fort Yellowstone in Yellowstone Park.

CURIOUS ART OF MAKING CAMPAIGN BANNERS.
AN IMPORTANT INDUSTRY THAT SPRINGS INTO LIFE ONLY ONCE IN FOUR YEARS.
Photographs by our staff photographer, T. C. Marler. See opposite page.

Making campaign banners became big business every four years. This picture shows how those banners were made in 1904.

This cartoon depicts the prohibition issue in 1904, which remained an emotional and controversial issue until its repeal in 1932. Note the evil appearance of the brewer as contrasted with the innocence of the mother and children.

Ralph E. Becker Collection

Ultimately, enough Republicans and Democrats wore enough buttons for prohibition to pass into law. Many politicians won or lost their elections because of their stand on liquor.

Ralph E. Becker Collection

83

1908

President: Republicans **William H. Taft** Democrats William Jennings Bryan
Vice-President: **James S. Sherman** John W. Kern

BORN SEPT. 15, 1857.
GRADUATED YALE, 1878.
ADMITTED TO BAR, 1880.
ASST. PROSECUTING
ATTY., 1881-'82.
COLLECTOR, INTERNAL
REVENUE, 1882-'83.
ASST. COUNTY
SOLICITOR, 1885-'87.
MARRIED 1886.
JUDGE SUPERIOR COURT
OF OHIO, 1887-90.

SOLICITOR GENERAL
OF U.S., 1890-'92.
JUDGE UNITED STATES
CIRCUIT COURT, 1892-1900.
PRESIDENT OF PHILIPPINE
COMMISSION, 1900-'04.
GOVERNOR OF
PHILIPPINES, 1901-'04.
SECRETARY OF WAR, 1904-08.
TOURED THE WORLD, 1907.
PRESIDENT, 1909.

Since the popular Teddy Roosevelt had stated publicly that he was bound by the two-term presidential tradition, he was not a candidate in 1908. He was to regret this later in life, but at this time he supported his own Secretary of War, William Howard Taft. Taft is shown here as very much a family man with his wife and three children.

The Republican National Convention was held in Chicago beginning on June 16. This shows the type of parading that was done by the delegates at this time.

The midwest Republicans had confidence in the Ohio-born William Howard Taft. He is shown here in a dignified pose on his campaign plate. Although he had not been an elected public servant, his appointment to Roosevelt's cabinet as Secretary of War kept his name in the public eye.

This hand-painted campaign banner was used by Taft supporters before and after his easy victory at the Republican National Convention. Taft's strong support by Teddy Roosevelt, the Party darling, won him the nomination.

Many watch fobs bore pictures of Taft. This was a novelty item, which many men of the day could and did wear.

This tin campaign tray showed the Republican candidates who had run for office from 1856 through 1908. Pictured on the tray with Mr. Taft was his vice-presidential candidate, James S. Sherman, Congressman from New York.

This picture, titled *The Chief Contestants*, showed the candidates who ran in 1908. The chief opposition to the Republican Party was once-again Democrat William Jennings Bryan, but the silver-tongued orator was doomed to still another defeat.

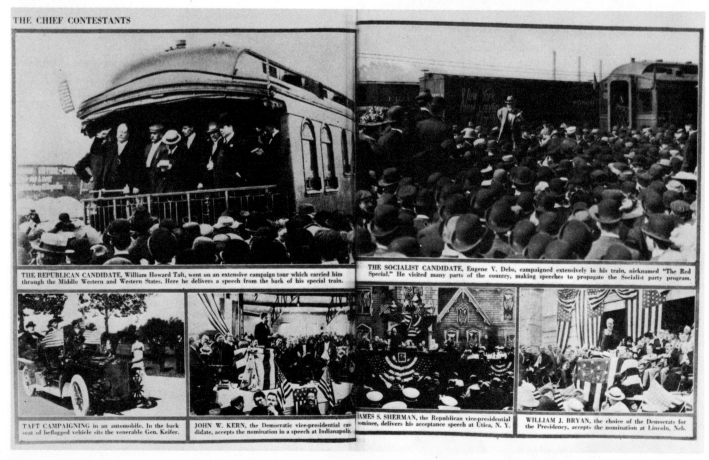

THE CHIEF CONTESTANTS

THE REPUBLICAN CANDIDATE, William Howard Taft, went on an extensive campaign tour which carried him through the Middle Western and Western States. Here he delivers a speech from the back of his special train.

THE SOCIALIST CANDIDATE, Eugene V. Debs, campaigned extensively in his train, nicknamed "The Red Special." He visited many parts of the country, making speeches to propagate the Socialist party program.

TAFT CAMPAIGNING in an automobile. In the back seat of beflagged vehicle sits the venerable Gen. Keifer.

JOHN W. KERN, the Democratic vice-presidential candidate, accepts the nomination in a speech at Indianapolis.

JAMES S. SHERMAN, the Republican vice-presidential nominee, delivers his acceptance speech at Utica, N. Y.

WILLIAM J. BRYAN, the choice of the Democrats for the Presidency, accepts the nomination at Lincoln, Neb.

Mr. Taft is shown here boarding a train at
Union Station in Washington, D.C. The solidity of
his figure—he was a large, heavy-set
man—impressed people who saw him.

By 1908, campaign methods included the use
of the comparatively new phonograph. Both
candidates are shown here with signs stating that
their speeches are available on the phonograph.

NATIONAL PLATFORM OF THE PROHIBITION PARTY

Adopted Columbus, Ohio, July 16, 1908

The Prohibition Party of the United States, assembled in convention at Columbus, Ohio, July 15-16, 1908, expressing gratitude to almighty God for the victories of our principles in the past, for encouragement at present, and for confidence in early and triumphant success in the future, makes the following declaration of principles, and pledges their enactment into law when placed in power:

1. The submission by Congress to the several states, of an amendment to the federal constitution prohibiting the manufacture, sale, importation, exportation or transportation of alcoholic liquors for beverage purposes.

2. The immediate prohibition of the liquor traffic for beverage purposes in the District of Columbia, in the territories and all places over which the national government has jurisdiction; the repeal of the internal revenue tax on alcoholic liquors and the prohibition of interstate traffic therein.

3. The election of United States Senators by direct vote of the people.

4. Equitable graduated income and inheritance taxes.

5. The establishment of postal savings banks and the guaranty of deposits in banks.

6. The regulation of all corporations doing an interstate commerce business.

7. The creation of a permanent tariff commission.

8. The strict enforcement of law instead of official tolerance and practical license of the social evil which prevails in many of our cities, with its unspeakable traffic in girls.

9. Uniform marriage and divorce laws.

10. An equitable and constitutional employers' liability act.

11. Court review of postoffice department decisions.

12. The prohibition of child labor in mines, workshops and factories.

13. Legislation basing suffrage only upon intelligence and ability to read and write the English language.

14. The preservation of the mineral and forest resources of the country, and the improvement of the highways and waterways.

Believing in the righteousness of our cause and the final triumph of our principles, and convinced of the unwillingness of the Republican and Democratic parties to deal with these issues, we invite to full party fellowship all citizens who are with us agreed.

Ralph E. Becker Collection

The Prohibition Party, in its own words, was "convinced of the unwillingness of the Republican and Democratic Parties to deal with these issues." While the prohibition of the sale of alcoholic liquors for beverage purposes was its main plank, this party also favored such ideas as the election of U.S. senators by direct vote of the people. The fourteen planks listed in the small print make interesting reading—and many Republicans did indeed read them.

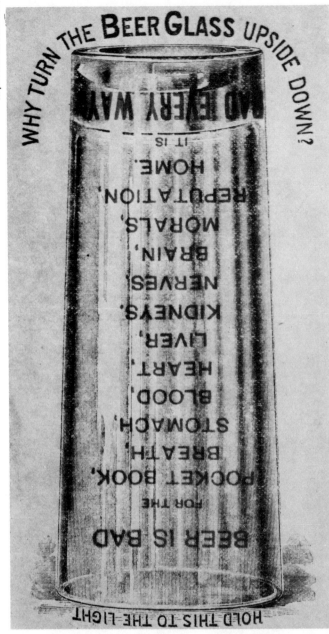

Novelty beer glasses, such as the one pictured here, were circulated for the cause of prohibition. Beer and whiskey were opposed by the "drys," and this opposition ultimately passed the prohibition law in this country. The issue was gaining momentum and was to become a major problem for both parties.

Temperance buttons were well circulated throughout the country at this time. Emotional appeals like this were what caused the Prohibition Admendment to be passed in 1919.

	Republicans	Democrats	Progressive (Bull Moose)
President:	William H. Taft	**Woodrow Wilson**	Theodore Roosevelt
Vice-President:	James S. Sherman	**Thomas R. Marshall**	Hiram W. Johnson

When the Republicans convened at the Coliseum in Chicago in 1912, two political friends parted company. Taft, who had worked well with Teddy Roosevelt in 1908, now stood alone.

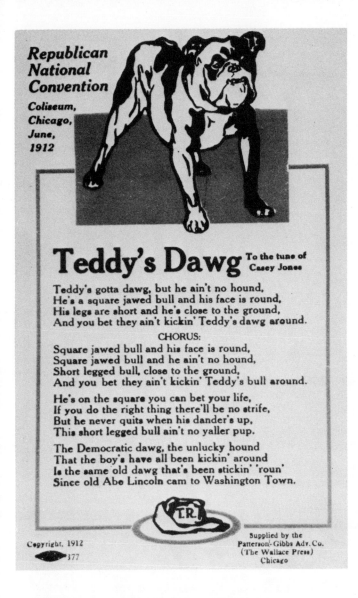

Teddy's gotta dawg, but he ain't no hound,
He's a square jawed bull and his face is round,
His legs are short and he's close to the ground,
And you bet they ain't kickin' Teddy's dawg around.

CHORUS:
Square jawed bull and his face is round,
Square jawed bull and he ain't no hound,
Short legged bull, close to the ground,
And you bet they ain't kickin' Teddy's bull around.

He's on the square you can bet your life,
If you do the right thing there'll be no strife,
But he never quits when his dander's up,
This short legged bull ain't no yaller pup.

The Democratic dawg, the unlucky hound
That the boy's have all been kickin' around
Is the same old dawg that's been stickin' 'roun'
Since old Abe Lincoln cam to Washington Town.

William Howard Taft won the nomination of the Republican Party for president. His victory, which was chiefly from the state machines of the East and Midwest, caused Roosevelt to gather his own forces by means of a third party—the Progressives. The split in the Republican Party gave the Democrats the advantage they needed and certainly helped to put Woodrow Wilson into office.

Taft was a conservative politician while Roosevelt was progressive, and the two candidates resorted to name-calling as they tried for the nomination. Although "Teddy's Dawg" was sung in Chicago in June, the slate for the 1912 election was to be Taft and Sherman.

The Progressive Party held a convention in Chicago on August 5 and nominated Roosevelt for the presidency and Governor Hiram Johnson of California for vice-president. Although this sheet music says, "In the stretch, 'Teddy' wins," Roosevelt was not destined to return to the White House.

TEDDY'S COMIN' BACK AGIN

(OUR NEXT PRESIDENT)
(By Capt. A. T. Hendricks)

The Latest Campaign Song Hit of the Season

"IN THE STRETCH" "TEDDY" WINS.

He Smiles and Fights On.

Not an Experiment, but the Greatest Living American.

Price 20 Cents

For Sale by Music Dealers Everywhere

Woodrow Wilson, Democratic candidate for president, campaigned vigorously, as did Taft and Roosevelt. But the third hat in the ring (Roosevelt's) divided what had been a united Republican Party, and Wilson went to the White House.

This postcard shows a typical scene in the Kentucky Mountains, when the men went to vote. Note that the wide street is just a dirt road and that many of the men wore hats. The absence of women in the scene shows that they still had not gained the right to vote.

This suffrage marching costume appeared in a Chicago parade in the early 1900s. The marching lady in pants was very racy for her time. Her costume and cause ultimately impressed both of the major parties.

Pictured here on a postcard, the Suffragettes' Parade marched through Washington, D.C., on March 13, 1913. The women were demanding enfranchisement from both parties, and amendment floats such as this called attention to their demands.

The women wanted the Republicans as well as the Democrats to pay attention to their demands. This suffrage parade left New York City on a pilgrimage to Washington, D.C. The women made so much noise that the men of the major parties were finally beginning to listen.

	Republicans	Democrats
President:	Charles E. Hughes	**Woodrow Wilson**
Vice-President:	Charles W. Fairbanks	**Thomas R. Marshall**

Ralph E. Becker Collection

Supreme Court Justice Charles E. Hughes of New York had refused to enter the state primaries for the Republican Party. However, the distinguished gentleman accepted the nomination when it came to him at the Republican National Convention in Chicago. Former Vice-President Fairbanks ran with Hughes as his running mate.

This campaign fan shows the Republican and Democratic candidates for 1916. The Democrats used a popular slogan—"He kept us out of war"—and this may have tipped the voting scales in favor of Wilson.

95

Although they belonged to different political parties, Hughes and Wilson had many things in common. They had both been college professors and governors of their respective states, and both men brought a dignity to their campaigning. Once he accepted the nomination for the presidency, Hughes campaigned vigorously on his own behalf.

At last the Republicans listened, and their candidate spoke out strongly for woman's suffrage. There are many women in this audience listening to Mr. Hughes' campaign promises. The umbrellas were probably raised against the hot sun rather than as protection from rain.

Whistle-stop campaigning was still a popular and expedient way to meet the people. Hughes covered many campaign miles this way but was not strong enough in the end to compete with Wilson's personality.

PREPAREDNESS—PROTECTION—PROSPERITY

FOR AUDITOR-GENERAL
CHARLES A. SNYDER

FOR UNITED STATES SENATOR
PHILANDER C. KNOX

FOR STATE TREASURER
HARMON M. KEPHART

FOR PRESIDENT
CHARLES E. HUGHES

FOR VICE-PRESIDENT
CHARLES W. FAIRBANKS

FOR CONGRESSMAN-AT-LARGE
THOMAS S. CRAGO

FOR CONGRESSMAN-AT-LARGE
MAHLON M. GARLAND

FOR CONGRESSMAN-AT-LARGE
JOSEPH McLAUGHLIN

FOR CONGRESSMAN-AT-LARGE
JOHN R. K. SCOTT

REPUBLICAN CANDIDATES
ELECTION TUESDAY, NOVEMBER 7, 1916

As this poster shows, election day was November 7. The popular Republican slogans, "Preparedness," "Protection," "Prosperity," were not enough to carry the election. The voters chose to remain with Woodrow Wilson.

The Victorian viewpoint of this cartoon was still held by many men in 1916. Men believed women were qualified to teach their children but not to vote. However, the petition for equal suffrage did not have much further to go.

Wilson kept the country out of war during his first term of office, but it was an impossibility after his reelection. This poster from World War I was intended to arouse the country into a definite home-front effort in order to give support to the "boys" who had gone to fight the war, known to some as "Mr. Wilson's War."

Demonstrations like this one in front of the White House forced the politicians to act on behalf of woman's suffrage.

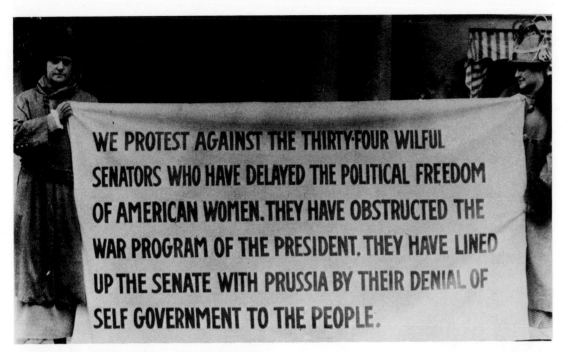

WE PROTEST AGAINST THE THIRTY-FOUR WILFUL SENATORS WHO HAVE DELAYED THE POLITICAL FREEDOM OF AMERICAN WOMEN. THEY HAVE OBSTRUCTED THE WAR PROGRAM OF THE PRESIDENT. THEY HAVE LINED UP THE SENATE WITH PRUSSIA BY THEIR DENIAL OF SELF GOVERNMENT TO THE PEOPLE.

The women did not stop in their efforts to gain the vote. This sign was held by National Women's Party pickets against the thirty-four senators who delayed the political freedom of American women in 1918.

Enough suffrage buttons were worn and enough noise was made so that Congress passed the Nineteenth Amendment in 1919, and women had won their long battle for the right to vote. Both Republicans and Democrats were forced to give their approval to this amendment, and it was ratified by all of the states in the summer of 1920. Women would vote in the coming national election.

1920

	Republicans	Democrats
President:	Warren G. Harding	James M. Cox
Vice-President:	Calvin Coolidge	Franklin D. Roosevelt

The candidates nominated in Chicago at the Republican National Convention were Warren G. Harding, Senator from Ohio, and Governor Calvin Coolidge of Massachusetts. The ideas of putting "America First" and getting back to normalcy after the devastating effects of World War I were foremost in Republican minds. The Republicans blamed the Democrats and Wilson for the "war to end all wars."

This delegation from the newly formed League of Women Voters attended both the Democratic and Republican National Conventions. The Republican Party accepted only five of the six planks shown here, omitting the public health and morals plank, which read, "Continued appropriation for public education and sex hygiene." This was considered a serious oversight on the part of the Republicans, as this plank was believed to make the strongest appeal to women.

Advertising such as this bicycle ad was used to keep the names of the Republican Party candidates in front of the people in a homey way. The idea was that if candidate Harding once rode a bike, he was a down-to-earth person. And Mr. Coolidge's son John, Jr. owned a 1920 bicycle too.

The fine print on this ad by the Republican National Committee creates a portrait of Warren G. Harding, the simple man. It talks of his "beautiful and simple family life in his modest Marion home, where his neighbors are his boyhood friends." It also says he is "the stuff that makes the true public servant."

The nose-thumber campaign novelty shown here on its original sales card was popular in the campaign of 1920. Can you find three Mr. Hardings thumbing their noses at the Democrats?

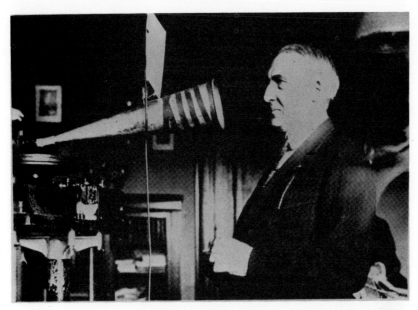

Harding, like McKinley before him, campaigned from his own front porch in Marion, Ohio. Here, he is shown recording one of his speeches for the phonograph-buying public.

Although he did win the election of 1920, Warren G. Harding did not live to serve out his term. He died in San Francisco on August 2, 1923, with his wife at his side. At that time, Calvin Coolidge took the oath of office for the presidency from his father in Vermont, with eight witnesses to the event. The ex-governor of Massachusetts was now the president of the United States.

103

1924

President:
Vice-President:

Republicans
Calvin Coolidge
Charles G. Dawes

Democrats
John W. Davis
Charles W. Bryan

Calvin Coolidge, once governor of Massachusetts, took over the presidency on the death of Warren Harding in 1923. This phonograph record of an early speech he made while governor was entitled "Law and Order." He said, "Change not the law but the attitude of the mind." His ideas along these lines continued into his terms as president.

The Republican Party liked Coolidge, the man. His attitude called to mind hard work, frugality, and honesty. He was a stern native of Vermont and a great contrast to his easy-going predecessor, President Harding. The campaign decal shown here reflected the Party attitudes—they wanted "Silent Cal."

The Republican National Convention was held in Cleveland, Ohio, and began on June 10. The Party platform favored tax reduction and came out against the League of Nations but for the World Court.

The winning presidential candidates shown on this official campaign song cover were Calvin Coolidge and General Charles G. Dawes of Illinois. Dawes was a down-to-earth banker whose favorite expletive was "Hell 'n Maria." He had served as purchasing agent for the American Expeditionary Forces during World War I and had served in politics for many years.

"KEEP COOL AND KEEP COOLIDGE"

HOME TOWN
COOLIDGE CLUB
PLYMOUTH, VERMONT

TO THE MEN AND WOMEN OF OUR COUNTRY:

In the early spring of this year in the building where President Calvin Coolidge was born, in a hall just above the room where he first saw the light of day, about fifty residents of Plymouth met and organized THE HOME TOWN COOLIDGE CLUB.

These pictures show the story of his life from the farm to the White House. It is a wonderful story of progress and development. This remarkable career had its origin in the homely virtues implanted by the simple life of the Vermont home which constitutes the background of his career.

In 1920 Speaker Gillette in presenting him as candidate for President said:

"A boyhood on a lonely farm in Vermont bred in him frugality and self-reliance. The granite hills seem to have moulded his great indomitable character. Family self-denial gave him a college education at Amherst which broadened his native talents. His neighbors recognized the value of this quiet, sagacious man, and drafted him into public service, and he glided from one useful station to another, until he reached the highest office of our State. He is not showy or spectacular, but he never disappoints. The limelight attracts him less than the midnight oil. He is patient as Lincoln, silent as Grant, diplomatic as McKinley, with the political instinct of Roosevelt. His character is as firm as the mountains of his native State."

The Coolidge Club of Plymouth, Vermont—Coolidge's hometown—supported Coolidge with glowing words. This letter describes the man as being "patient as Lincoln, silent as Grant, diplomatic as McKinley with the political instinct of Roosevelt."

106

The official campaign song of the Home Town Coolidge Club reiterated the Republican Party slogan, "Keep Cool and Keep Coolidge."

Ralph E. Becker Collection

This banner flew from one of the official cars the candidates used while on a speaking tour in 1924. In addition to the popularity of their candidates, Coolidge and Dawes, the Republicans benefited from the fact that business was good and the country prosperous.

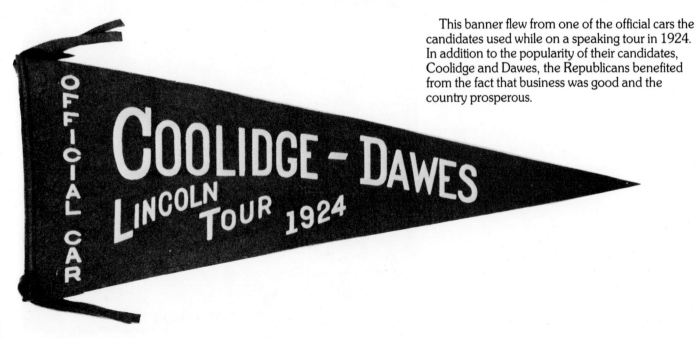

This Coolidge stamp was put out by the state of Wisconsin. The idea of keeping cool with Coolidge went along with the idea of keeping cool in Wisconsin.

The Coolidge Lamp and Bible presented "Old Cal" as one of the common people—an impression that was stressed throughout his time in public office. The gracious and friendly attitude of his wife, Grace, offset the austerity of the man himself.

	Republicans	Democrats
President:	Herbert C. Hoover	Alfred E. Smith
Vice-President:	Charles Curtis	Joseph T. Robinson

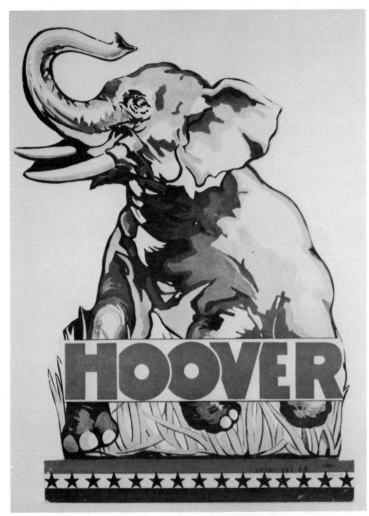

Ralph E. Becker Collection

After Coolidge's famous announcement that said "I do not choose to run," the Republican Party chose "the great engineer" from Iowa, Herbert Clark Hoover, for their presidential candidate in 1928. His running mate was Senator Charles Curtis of Kansas.

Window posters, like this one put out by the Women's Committee for Hoover, were seen all over the country. Although Hoover had differences with Coolidge and lacked the President's support, he captured the Party nomination with a strong stand supporting prohibition and promising friendliness to agriculture.

A happy Republican must have placed this Hoover hat on the bust of Democratic candidate Al Smith. Hoover and Smith were miles apart on campaign issues, and the campaign waged was a bloody one.

License plates for both Republican and Democratic candidates were frequently displayed. These metal tags have been replaced in modern campaigning with automobile bumper stickers.

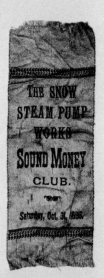

Hoover supporters also used posters like the one shown here as a means of keeping the candidate's face and name before the public.

THIS HOME IS FOR
HOOVER

Humanizing Herbert Hoover was a political necessity. This picture of Mr. Hoover fishing shows the politician relaxing like just plain folks.

The "Wets" or anti-Prohibitionists were wearing repeal pins like this one during the 1928 presidential campaign. Hoover was in strong support of the enforcement of the prohibition law. Although prohibition had a few more years to remain as the law of the land, it was on its way out.

This is a mild sample of the mudslinging that went on during the campaign of 1928. Here, the Republicans point a finger at the ethnic and religious background of Al Smith. Smith's money was labeled "hooie and hokum," and a pot shot was taken at the derby that Smith usually wore.

	Republicans	Democrats
President:	Herbert C. Hoover	Franklin D. Roosevelt
Vice-President:	Charles Curtis	John N. Garner

The Grand Old Party convened its National Convention in Chicago in June. The delegates prepared the planks for the Party, including one to change the Eighteenth Amendment to allow repeal of prohibition in those states that wanted it repealed. This plank was in contrast to the full repeal of prohibition promised by the Democrats.

Herbert Hoover was again nominated for the presidential slot and insisted upon Curtis as his vice-president.

"KEEP THEM ON THE JOB"

HERBERT HOOVER
Republican Candidate for President

CHARLES CURTIS
Republican Candidate for Vice-President

Ralph E. Becker Collection

This Hoover-Curtis campaign poster shows formal pictures of the candidates as well as the Republican wish to "Keep them on the job."

REPUBLICAN

This automobile attachment was used by party devotees in the 1930s. By this time, the elephant was the acknowledged symbol of the Republican Party, as it still is today.

Although there was not as much money in the campaign till as there had been in more prosperous campaigns, this silk broadside was printed to show the virtues of President Hoover. Note that the Republicans of Pennsylvania were strongly for the cancellation of the Eighteenth Amendment.

Both Republicans and Democrats used political bandannas as campaign gimmicks. These two bandannas are almost identical, with the exception of the picture in the center and the lettering under each picture.

This Republican broadside was aimed at the Democratic vice-presidential candidate, "Postoffice Jack" Garner. It stressed the idea of extravagant spending by the Democrats.

FIRST the HAM; THEN the HOG!

THE $6,000 HAM	THE $55,000 HOG

The old postoffice in Uvalde, Tex., which was replaced by a $55,000 one through efforts of Speaker Garner.	The new $55,000 postoffice in Uvalde, Tex., home town of Speaker Garner, Democratic vice presidential candidate.

"Postoffice Jack" Garner's billion dollar pork barrel scheme to bring back prosperity by going broke was the culmination of 17 years feeding at the pork barrel trough. As far back as 1915 the Uvalde, Texas, Democrat raided the treasury to build unneeded postoffices in his district.

In a speech at the Atascosa, Texas, fair in that year he said:

"There are a half dozen places in my district where Federal buildings are being erected or have recently been constructed at a cost to the Government far in excess of the actual needs of the communities where they are located.

"Take Uvalde, my own home town, for instance. We are putting up a Post Office down there at a cost of $60,000 when a $5,000 building would be entirely adequate for our needs.... I'll tell you right now *every time one of those Yankees gets a ham, I'm going to do my best to get a hog.*"

A Vote for Garner and Roosevelt is a Vote for More Unneeded Hogs

VOTE FOR HOOVER, CURTIS AND PROSPERITY

Issued by
REPUBLICAN NATIONAL COMMITTEE
Palmer House, Chicago, Ill.

Although Herbert Hoover was not the speaker, this rally took place on his behalf at Ripon, Wisconsin, the birthplace of the Republican Party. The building in the background is the schoolhouse where the first Republicans met in 1854.

Both Hoover and Roosevelt made speeches on the radio that reached into the homes of America. However, because Mr. Hoover could not compete with the easy oratory of F.D.R., he had to get out and talk directly with the people, as he is doing here at Madison Square Garden.

Hoover campaigned by train with frequent whistle-stops along the way. Crowds did gather wherever the train stopped.

This Republican street rally shows a sign used repeatedly by the Republicans, which said "We want to turn the corner to prosperity." However, the nation did not buy this idea and favored the new paths proposed by F.D.R., who won the election of 1932 in a big way.

Equal Rights

VOL. XVIII, No. 32
FIVE CENTS

SATURDAY
SEPTEMBER 10, 1932

Alice Paul

Leader of the Feminist movement in America and commonly regarded as one of the greatest of living statesmen, Alice Paul, with other Feminists of world-wide renown, is in Geneva urging the re-drafting of the proposed code of international law to be administered by the World Court of the League of Nations. The present draft contains discriminations in nationality against women. The Feminist demand is not only for an initial codification that shall be "founded on justice," but also that means shall be provided "for taking into consideration the woman's point of view on all codification projects affecting the status of women which may hereafter be brought forward."

An interesting sidelight on the election of 1932 was the action of the women. They were now publishing a magazine called "Equal Rights" on behalf of the National Woman's Party. Alice Paul was the leader of the feminist movement of that time. These women were the aunts and mothers of future ERA fighters.

1936

	Republicans	Democrats
President:	Alfred M. Landon	Franklin D. Roosevelt
Vice-President:	Frank Knox	John N. Garner

The National Republican Convention was held in Cleveland, Ohio, in June, and the man of the hour was Governor Alfred M. Landon of Kansas. The party platform called for relief from unemployment, a balanced budget, and collective bargaining in labor disputes, but it was a platform of generalities rather than specifics.

This convention portrait of Alf Landon showed the Governor as a serious-minded public figure much along the lines of the serious Coolidge of earlier days. The Landon backers felt that their candidate would run well, as he came from the center of the farm belt and could bring in needed votes from that section of the country.

VOTE FOR LANDON AND KNOX

ALF M. LANDON
Republican Candidate for President

COL. FRANK KNOX
Republican Candidate for Vice-President

Ralph E. Becker Collection

The winners at the Republican Convention were Landon and Knox. Colonel Frank Knox was the publisher of the Chicago Daily News, and it was his determined pre-convention campaigning that earned him the place of vice-president on the Republican ballot.

The fear of "New Deal" spending was frequently mentioned by both Landon and Knox in their campaign speeches. Banners such as this one were in evidence wherever they spoke.

121

Pennants were popular in 1936, and this felt pennant with the GOP elephant and the candidates names on it is typical of the ones made at that time.

Sheet music was still a popular method of spreading the candidate's name. This was the official Republican campaign song, and phonograph records of the song could be purchased from the publisher at 50 cents each.

"Elect Landon, Save America" was imprinted on the Alf Landon punch glass found in Republican homes in this election year. Many a toast must have been raised to the Republican candidate who planned to right all the wrongs the Democrats had caused.

The comparison of Lincoln with Landon may have seemed strange to some, but the men holding this banner believed that the prairie governor could win the presidency.

THE DOLLAR IN HOG-FARMING

The cartoonist shows Landon on the fence about the farm issue. F.D.R. had provided farm subsidies during his first term of office. The Republicans could not compete with this, nor could the men of big business who backed them. Roosevelt won the election by a landslide and returned to office for a second term.

	Republicans	Democrats
President:	Wendell L. Willkie	Franklin D. Roosevelt
Vice-President:	Charles L. McNary	Henry A. Wallace

Prior to the Republican National Convention in Philadelphia in June of 1940, the cry "We Want Willkie" was heard all over the country. Willkie clubs were springing up in support of the Indiana native, who had proved himself an able businessman in New York City. Willkie's humor, reminiscent of that of Will Rogers, and his pleasing personality gave him tremendous popular support.

THE REPUBLICAN 1940 VICTORY TICKET

VOTE FOR THEM AND
**PHILADELPHIA COUNTY
REPUBLICAN CANDIDATES**

For Congress

1st DISTRICT
EMANUEL W. BELOFF

2nd DISTRICT
AUGUSTUS TRASK ASHTON

3rd DISTRICT
FRANK J. KOWNACKI

4th DISTRICT
BENJAMIN M. GOLDER

5th DISTRICT
FRED C. GARTNER

6th DISTRICT
FRANK F. TRUSCOTT

7th DISTRICT
HUGH D. SCOTT, Jr.

Vote the REPUBLICAN TICKET Nov. 5th

The Republican victory ticket included Willkie as the presidential candidate and Senator McNary of Oregon as vice-president. McNary, who had supported a number of New Deal measures, was chosen as a liberal from the West. It was hoped that by choosing McNary, the party ticket would be strengthened and ultimately win.

MR. and MRS. WENDELL L. WILLKIE

Mr. and Mrs. Willkie were both pleasant people and well received wherever they appeared. Willkie was a good speaker, who came out for his ideas honestly and frankly. On foreign policy, he did not differ much from the Democratic candidate and upheld the Republican Party Plank to act for "peoples fighting for liberty."

Although the law of the land did not prevent F.D.R. from running for a third term of office as president, there was a no third-term tradition. Willkie supporters shouted loudly that they did not want Roosevelt for a third term, as shown on this automobile license tag attachment.

Europe was a war-torn battlefield in 1940, with Hitler taking over country after country. This Republican poster showed a French soldier blaming politicians for the fact he was no longer free. The Willkie War Veterans National Committee implied that Willkie would be the man to keep Americans free.

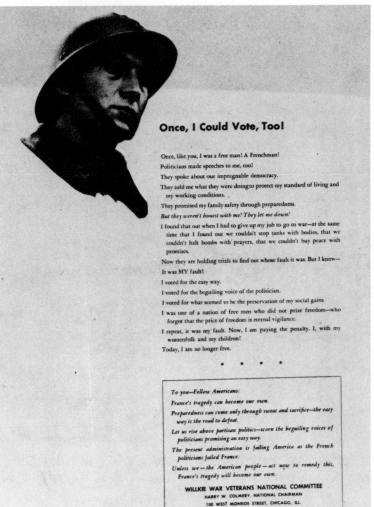

Once, I Could Vote, Too!

Once, like you, I was a free man! A Frenchman!

Politicians made speeches to me, too!

They spoke about our impregnable democracy.

They told me what they were doing to protect my standard of living and my working conditions.

They promised my family safety through preparedness.

But they weren't honest with me! They let me down!

I found that out when I had to give up my job to go to war—at the same time that I found out we couldn't stop tanks with bodies, that we couldn't halt bombs with prayers, that we couldn't buy peace with promises.

Now they are holding trials to find out whose fault it was. But I know—

It was MY fault!

I voted for the easy way.

I voted for the beguiling voice of the politician.

I voted for what seemed to be the preservation of my social gains.

I was one of a nation of free men who did not prize freedom—who forgot that the price of freedom is eternal vigilance.

I repeat, it was my fault. Now, I am paying the penalty. I, with my womenfolk and my children!

Today, I am no longer free.

* * * * *

To you—Fellow Americans:

France's tragedy can become our own.

Preparedness can come only through sweat and sacrifice—the easy way is the road to defeat.

Let us rise above partisan politics—scorn the beguiling voices of politicians promising an easy way.

The present administration is failing America as the French politicians failed France.

Unless we—the American people—act now to remedy this, France's tragedy will become our own.

WILLKIE WAR VETERANS NATIONAL COMMITTEE
HARRY W. COLMERY, NATIONAL CHAIRMAN
100 WEST MONROE STREET, CHICAGO, ILL.

This collection of campaign buttons shows the many areas in which Willkie had support. Young people were very active in Willkie's behalf, even though those under twenty-one years old could not vote. The idea of no third term was put on many buttons, and election day was called "Dethronement Day."

1

2

1. Abraham Lincoln of Illinois was the first Republican candidate to win the office of president of the United States. The Lincoln pictured here is a younger and more vigorous man than was shown in later pictures of him.

2. This wooden hatchet was used in an 1860 Lincoln parade and symbolized Lincoln's humble beginnings. He had chopped wood as a boy in Illinois, and this image superceded that of the lawyer and politician who was to lead the nation during most of the Civil War.

3. This 1884 canvass book was used on behalf of the Republican candidates for casting the voters' ballots. Voters of 1884 would be as confused by modern voting machines as we would be by this now-outdated system.

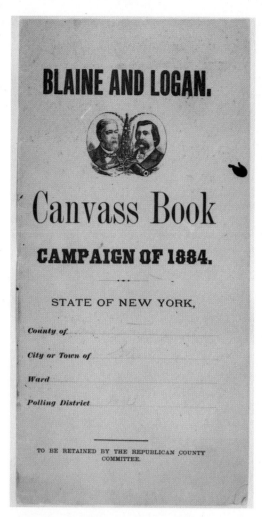

BLAINE AND LOGAN.

Canvass Book

CAMPAIGN OF 1884.

STATE OF NEW YORK,

County of

City or Town of

Ward

Polling District

TO BE RETAINED BY THE REPUBLICAN COUNTY COMMITTEE.

4. Although the Republicans did not win the election of 1884, they put out a lot of campaign material. This patriotic poster featured Blaine and Logan.

FOR PRESIDENT
JAMES G. BLAINE.
OF MAINE

FOR VICE PRESIDENT
JOHN A. LOGAN.
OF ILLINOIS.

5. The biblical allusion here is to the first names of the Republican candidates for the presidency and vice-presidency in 1888. BENJAMIN Harrison of Indiana and LEVI P. Morton of New York carried the party banner that year.

6. The Republican nominees won the election in 1896, and McKinley took up residence at 1600 Pennsylvania Avenue.

7. This 1900 campaign poster showed how prosperous the country had been under McKinley's guidance. The words under the candidates' pictures are intended to justify the Spanish-American War issue.

8. The sheet music shown here on behalf of Teddy Roosevelt declares it was sung "in all the leading Vaudeville Houses." Although Mr. Roosevelt did not favor the caricatures of himself, the public enjoyed his idiosyncrasies as well as his hearty manner.

d

9. The presidential Republican candidate in 1928 was Herbert C. Hoover, known by many as the ''great engineer.'' Banners like the one pictured here were prominent wherever Republicans assembled.

10. Alf M. Landon of Kansas ran against Franklin D. Roosevelt in 1936. However, Governor Landon lost the election, and F.D.R. went back to the White House for a second term.

e

WIN WITH

WILLKIE
BROOCH

11. "Win with Willkie" was a slogan echoing all over the country in 1940. Willkie was tremendously popular because of his humor and pleasing personality, and he fought hard although unsuccessfully to defeat Roosevelt, who was running for his third term.

EXTREMISM IN THE DEFENSE OF LIBERTY IS NO VICE; MODERATION IN THE PURSUIT OF JUSTICE IS NO VIRTUE GOLDWATER IN '64

12. Barry Goldwater was called an extremist by many people in 1964. The slogan written on this campaign button shows how he felt about this charge.

f

13. Richard M. Nixon smiled broadly on this campaign poster of 1972. Despite democratic criticism of his foreign and domestic policies, the voters chose this long-time politician to lead the country as their president.

14. This colorful Reagan for President poster did not win the nomination for Governor Ronald Reagan of California. The delegates nominated Gerald R. Ford to succeed himself as president. The peanut with the smiling teeth represented Democratic candidate Jimmy Carter.

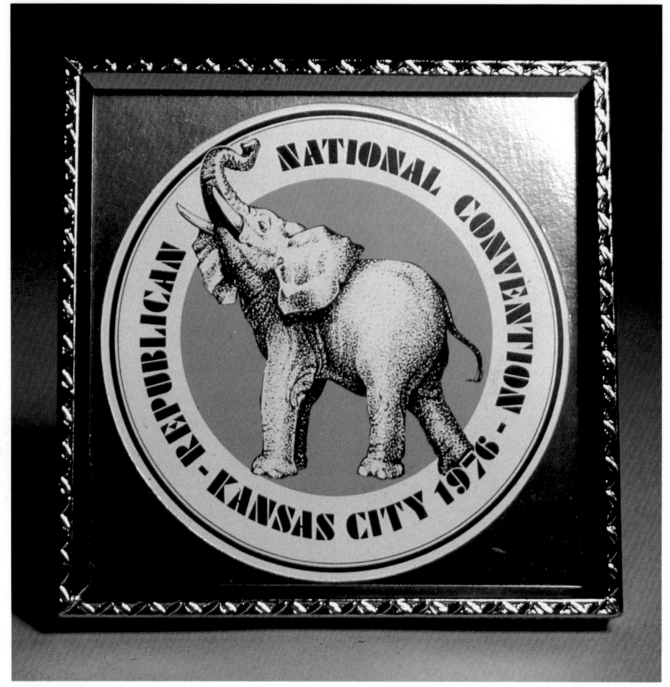

15. Souvenirs like this one were offered at the
Republican National Convention at Kansas City in
1976. The Republicans hoped the trumpeting
elephant would become a symbol of victory for the
Party.

"No Franklin the First," "Roosevelt for EX President," and "No Third Term" are only three of the many buttons issued by the Republicans. This was an emotional issue, because many feared that Roosevelt might become a dictator if he won another election.

The Works Progress Administration (W.P.A.) was a Democratic program begun under President Roosevelt. The Republicans were opposed to this program as shown by this campaign novelty. When the door was opened, a starved skeleton sat inside.

Wendell Willkie covered thirty-four states during his campaign and some thirty thousand miles by car, train, or plane. He seemed a tireless speaker and continued, even over the objections of his doctor, when his voice gave out. However, when the final vote was taken, Willkie lost out to the still-popular people's choice, President Roosevelt.

	Republicans	Democrats
President:	Thomas E. Dewey	Franklin D. Roosevelt
Vice-President:	John W. Bricker	Harry S. Truman

Governor Thomas E. Dewey of New York won the Republican nomination for president at the Republican National Convention in Chicago in June. Dewey and the party platform both promised that the war would be fought until victory was achieved. The platform further promised, "responsible participation by the United States in postwar cooperative organization."

In his acceptance speech for the nomination, Mr. Dewey said, "The future of America has no limit." The delegates cheered their candidate wildly.

The vice-presidential candidate for the Republicans was John W. Bricker, governor of Ohio. Bricker had been in nomination for the presidency but bowed out to Dewey and went on to accept the second spot on the ticket.

Dewey-Bricker
Madison Square Garden Rally
SATURDAY, NOVEMBER 4, 1944

No. 1—"STAR SPANGLED BANNER"

Oh! say, can you see, by the dawn's early light,
What so proudly we hailed at the twilight's last gleaming?
Whose broad stripes and bright stars, through the perilous night,
O'er the ramparts we watched, were so gallantly streaming;
And the rockets' red glare, the bombs bursting in air,
Gave proof through the night that our flag was still there.
Oh! say, does that star-spangled banner yet wave
O'er the land of the free and the home of the brave!

No. 2—"AMERICA"

My country, 'tis of thee,
Sweet land of liberty,
  Of thee I sing.
Land where my fathers died,
Land of the pilgrims' pride,
From every mountain side
  Let freedom ring.

Our fathers' God, to thee,
Author of liberty,
  To thee we sing.
Long may our land be bright
With freedom's holy light,
Protect us by Thy might,
  Great God our King!

No. 3—"GOD BLESS AMERICA"

God bless America, land that I love.
Stand beside her and guide her
Thru the night with a light from above.
From the mountains to the prairies
To the oceans white with foam
God bless America, my home, sweet home.

No. 4—Tune, "PUT ON YOUR OLD GRAY BONNET"

Put on your campaign bonnet,
Write VIC-TOR-Y upon it,
And we'll all go forward to the fray...
Oh, New York will be in clover
When we put Tom Curran over,
On our next election day.

No. 5—Tune of "OVER THERE"

Dewey there! Dewey there!
Sing it out, shout it out, Dewey there!
Let the nation hear it;
His friends will cheer it;
New Dealers fear it everywhere.
Dewey there! Dewey there!
In that old White House chair, that is where
We will seat him; naught defeat him.
Tell the whole wide world that Thomas
  Dewey's there.

No. 6—Tune of "GOOD NIGHT LADIES!"

Good night, Perkins,
Good night, Ickes,
Good night, Browder
You're leaving us at last.
Pack your grip and roll along, roll along,
  roll along,
Pack your grip and roll along.
(Slow) and—clearing—with—Sidney—is—past!

No. 7—Tune of "MY DARLING CLEMENTINE"

Do we need him, do we want him,
  Do we know that he'll come through,
Do we get him in the White House,
  You can bet your life we do.
    Chorus
  Vote for Dewey!
  Thomas Dewey!
  Here's a real American!
  Win with Dewey,
  Ray for Dewey,
  Thomas Dewey is our man!
In a medley of confusion
  Hazy dreams and schemes abound,
We are voting for a leader
  With his feet upon the ground.
Repeat chorus.

No. 8—Tune of "SWANEE RIVER"

1. Way down upon a dozen rivers,
    Texas to Maine,
   Where California sunshine quivers,
    Back in the Ozark lane.
      Chorus
   Seems like everyone is saying,
    Everywhere I roam,
   "We aim to vote for Thomas Dewey!
    "He's like our own folks at home!
2. All up and down this far-flung nation,
    That's why they say.
   All keyed to hopeful expectation,
    Waiting election day.   **Repeat Chorus.**

The songs shown on this song sheet from an important pre-election rally at Madison Square Garden created enthusiasm among those present. In song number 8, they sang out: "We aim to vote for Thomas Dewey! He's like our own folks at home!"

A Democratic campaign song sheet stressed the idea that Roosevelt was the man to re-re-re-elect. Neither the idea of a fourth term nor the fact that F.D.R. was in poor health stopped the Democrats from winning the election. The country did not want to change horses in midstream. They wanted President Roosevelt to lead them out of war and into a time of peace.

1944
CAMPAIGN SONG

━━ ★ ━━

LET'S
RE - RE - RE -ELECT
ROOSEVELT

━━ ★ ━━

A SNAPPY MARCH TUNE
Words That Mean Something

━━ ★ ━━

DEDICATED TO
THE COMMANDER - IN - CHIEF

FINGER LAKES PRESS, INC., AUBURN, N.Y.

VOTE

TRUMAN

FOR
PRESIDENT

Harry Truman was not to run for the office of president until 1948, when this campaign button appeared. However, he was sworn into office on April 12, 1945, at Warm Springs, Georgia, after the death of President Roosevelt. The little haberdashery man was now president of the United States.

	Republicans	Democrats
President:	Thomas E. Dewey	**Harry S. Truman**
Vice-President:	Earl Warren	**Alben W. Barkley**

THE OREGON DEBATE

REPUBLICAN OPPONENTS in Oregon's primary were Dewey and Stassen. The result was important to both, for this was the last test of strength before the convention.

Nevertheless, Congress adjourned, and two days later the Republican nominating convention opened in Philadelphia. Governor Dwight H. Green of Illinois delivered the keynote address, seen and heard over hundreds of thousands of television sets throughout the country. He abused the New Deal and the Democratic party, which was "held together by bosses, boodle, buncombe and blarney," and praised the record of the Eightieth Congress, which had restored faith in representative government, had freed American economy from regimentation, balanced the budget, reduced Federal income taxes, and corrected chaotic conditions in labor relations.

The attractive Clare Boothe Luce, the woman keynoter, made a far more interesting appeal to her audience, spicing it with wisecracks and witticisms. Mrs. Luce said that President Truman was "a gone goose," whose "time is short and whose situation is hopeless," and whose three years in office were not "the pause that refreshes." She told the convention that "Democratic Presidents are always troubadours of trouble, crooners of catastrophe; they cannot win elections except in the climate of crisis. So

CLIMAX OF THE OREGON CAMPAIGN was a radio debate between Dewey and Stassen in Portland on the theme: "Shall the Communist party be outlawed?" In the election Oregon Republicans backed Dewey, who won the state's 12 delegates. The Stassen bandwagon, which had rolled so briskly in the previous primaries, came to an abrupt halt.

The 1948 Oregon state primary election was an important one for the Republicans. The opponents were the still-Governor of New York, Thomas E. Dewey, and Harold E. Stassen of Minnesota. Dewey spent three weeks ardently campaigning for support in that test state and won the delegates to the National Convention. As a result, Stassen dropped out of the running.

135

THE SYMBOL. A fifteen-foot balloon-rubber elephant, which collapsed and had to be reinflated, decorated the hotel where Dewey had his headquarters.

AN ANGEL in the streets outside Earl Warren's headquarters was hardly noticed as she distributed the address of an eating place to convention crowds.

DEMONSTRATORS parade at night with banners through the streets of Philadelphia in an effort to boost enthusiasm for their candidate, Harold E. Stassen.

RIVALRY is displayed in the lobby of the Benjamin Franklin Hotel, where a huge portrait of Senator Vandenberg is posted below a picture of Robert A. Taft.

Philadelphia was a busy town when the Republican National Convention assembled in June. These scenes show the headquarters of four of the men being considered for the office of president. They were Thomas Dewey, Earl Warren, Harold E. Stassen (whose supporters were still active despite Oregon results), and Senator Vandenberg.

This close-up of Dewey headquarters at the Bellevue Stratford shows the fifteen-foot rubber elephant that decorated the hotel. At one point, the elephant collapsed but was soon reinflated for all to see.

Governor Dewey and Governor Earl Warren of California were the victors at the Philadelphia Republican Convention. Both men are shown here on various campaign buttons popular during the remainder of the presidential campaign.

THOMAS E. DEWEY
1948

Neckties like the one shown here were frequently worn by campaigning Republicans. Dewey was as personable and popular a candidate in '48 as he had been in '44.

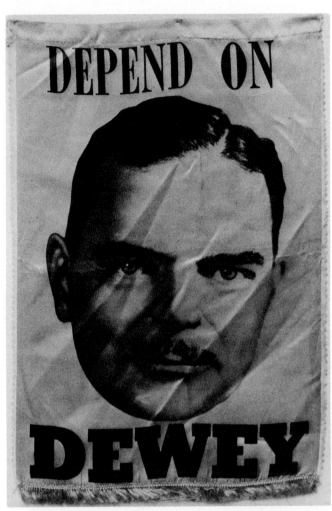

A man who had twice run and won the office of governor for the state of New York was indeed a man who could be depended upon. This banner was frequently displayed wherever Republicans gathered.

This Republican campaign sheet music of 1948 reminded Republicans of their roots with Abraham Lincoln. The elephant and the flag both salute Lincoln's picture.

Ralph E. Becker Collection

Dewey pennants were waved when Republicans promised a bipartisan foreign policy. Even civil rights were touched upon with a pledge of "equal opportunity to work."

The *Dewey Victory Special* traveled around the country with the candidate and his wife making frequent appearances.

Republicans Dewey and Warren, as well as Democrat Harry Truman, used the trains for campaigning. The polls seemed to indicate a Republican victory, but President Truman never stopped talking to the people.

THOMAS DEWEY conducted a lofty campaign, stressing the theme of unity and confining himself to generalities. He avoided any commitment to a specific program.

HARRY TRUMAN conducted an old-fashioned, slambang campaign, assailing the "do-nothing Republican Congress," and branding the GOP as the party of reaction.

sleeping on election day. You might call them sleeping polls."

Truman expanded on the theme. "These Republican polls are no accident. They are all part of a design to prevent a big vote on November 2 by convincing you that it makes no difference whether you vote or not. They want to do this because they know in their hearts that a big vote spells their defeat. They know that a big vote means a Democratic victory, because the Democratic party stands for the greatest good for the greatest number of the people."

Dewey, on the following day, told Clevelanders that "In the opening speech of this campaign at Des Moines, Iowa, I said this will be 'a campaign to unite America.' " Truman's campaign, however, was an attempt to split the nation.

The third round was in Boston, where Truman denounced as a "malicious falsehood" Re-

EARL WARREN, Dewey's running mate, made an impression wherever he spoke. Many felt he would have been a better presidential choice than the New Yorker.

This newspaper headline can never be forgotten by anyone who waited for election results in 1948. Harry Truman went to bed with Dewey in the lead for the popular vote, but, when he woke up on November 3, he was still President Harry S. Truman.

1952

President: Republicans — **Dwight D. Eisenhower** / Democrats — Adlai E. Stevenson
Vice-President: **Richard M. Nixon** / John J. Sparkman

General Eisenhower was serving in Europe as NATO commander when his name came up as a possible presidential candidate for the Republicans. "Ike," as he was popularly called, heeded the call and returned to the country in June of 1952 declaring his intention to run. The Draft-Ike movement had been a success.

Eisenhower pledged to end the Korean War, and his ability as a military figure in World War II helped him to victory in his campaign for the presidency. It is fitting that his first political speech was made in Abilene, Kansas, where he spent his boyhood.

Boyhood Home of General Eisenhower

ABILENE KANSAS

The Republican National Convention met in Chicago in July, and a platform was shaped that leaned toward states' rights and away from government interference in business. As a world figure, General Eisenhower had little trouble capturing the nomination for the presidency.

The delegates cheered loudly when Dwight David Eisenhower rose to accept the nomination. He may not have offered much political know-how but he did have warmth and sincerity.

FOR PRESIDENT

FOR VICE PRESIDENT

GOP

DWIGHT D. EISENHOWER

RICHARD M. NIXON

This newspaper broadside showing both of the party candidates appeared after the National Convention. Senator Nixon, thirty-nine years old from California, appealed to the youth of the country and was well known for his work on the House Un-American Activities Committee.

This picture shows the D.C. headquarters for Eisenhower and Nixon, and the men who were working on the campaign. The large elephant on the desk may have been cheering for the Republican slate.

Handkerchiefs like this Win with Ike bandanna were produced in large quantities. The engaging picture of Ike with his broad smile made it a favorite campaign memento.

The Republican women probably carried handkerchiefs like this dainty one pictured here. It may have been smaller than the bandanna above but it still carried the watchwords of the party—"I like Ike."

Campaign songs were sung for Eisenhower and Nixon, with a strong appeal made for the youth of the country. Eisenhower believed that if the youth understood the relationship between individual effort and common good, the future of the country was secure.

The *Eisenhower Special* covered many miles, and the speeches decried Democratic blunders in foreign policy as well as corruption in Washington. But perhaps the most incendiary issue was that of communist dangers within the country.

The Republicans touted their candidates by carrying many different pennants. This one showed the winning team of Eisenhower and Nixon, with a cheering elephant beside their pictures.

Cigarettes were smoked from packs with the running candidate's picture on them. The voter had his choice of Eisenhower or Democrat Adlai Stevenson. Unfortunately for Stevenson, he went up in smoke rather than to the White House.

Mamie and Ike were a personable couple and Mamie strongly supported her husband in his efforts to win. This political button was proudly worn by many staunch Republicans.

TOO CLOSE FOR COMFORT!

	OHIO	CALIFORNIA
Truman	1,452,791	1,913,134
Dewey	1,445,684	1,895,269
	7,107	17,865

DEPRESSION

MISSED US by only 12,487 Votes. If only 12,487 of 6,957,609 Voters in California and Ohio had switched to Dewey in 1948, Truman would have lost. Five million voters stayed home. Your State may decide this year's election results by a few votes.

Don't Gamble On Poverty with the GOP

STAY SAFE — VOTE STEVENSON

Labor's Committee for Stevenson and Sparkman

GEORGE M. HARRISON, *Chairman*   E. L. OLIVER, *Secretary-Treasurer*
1621 K Street, N.W., Washington 5, D. C.

In this broadside, the Democrats stressed the theme of getting out the vote. Past elections had been "too close for comfort." It was hoped that the winning figures would show the voter how important each vote was.

This clean-up bucket was needed when Richard Nixon had to defend himself against charges of corruption. He did ably defend himself in a television broadcast where he gave the history of his personal finances. He became famous for the mention of his wife's "respectable Republican cloth coat."

	Republicans	Democrats
President:	Dwight D. Eisenhower	Adlai E. Stevenson
Vice-President:	Richard M. Nixon	Estes Kefauver

The sheet music shown here was written by
Irving Berlin in support of Eisenhower for four more
years. The support was still strong despite the
President's heart attack in 1955 and his recent
surgery in June of 1956. The cry of the country was
"I still like Ike."

WITHHOLD NOT GOOD FROM THEM TO WHOM IT IS DUE, WHEN IT IS IN THE POWER OF THINE HAND TO DO IT.

PROVERBS 4: 27

YOUR VOTE
"IT'S DUE HIM IN '56"
VOTE FOR EISENHOWER

The National Republican Convention was held late in August in 1956, thereby shortening the campaign of the candidates. In a time when television brought those candidates right into the home, and planes made distances shorter, it was only reasonable for the Party to shorten the campaign time.

The health of the President did become an issue in this campaign, but the popularity of the man overcame this. The campaign poster shown here portrays a strong and vigorous man.

Ralph E. Becker Collection

Eisenhower political buttons were proudly worn all over the country. The Grand Old Party elephant was to carry the Republican slate back into the White House.

Although Eisenhower did not insist upon Nixon as his running mate, he was delighted when the Republicans renominated the younger man. Nixon campaigned vigorously and effectively, with Pat Nixon at his side.

Ralph E. Becker Collection

This Eisenhower badge pictures Ike and Mamie with broad smiles, as well as their home in Gettysburg. This home was usually called "the farm" and added to the folksy image of the Eisenhowers, although as pictured here the home is anything but small and humble.

Ralph E. Becker Collection

WE'VE HAD IT !

TO STEVENSON CAMP

COURTESY OF NORMAN IMPELMAN, S.F. CALIF.

This Democratic campaign sign was widely circulated but was not, in effect, true. There was a landslide victory for Ike as president. The Congress, however, went for a Democratic majority, thus giving a Republican president an opposition Congress.

Peace in Korea was the forerunner of the peace and prosperity that the Republicans promised the country. Here, President Eisenhower is seen reviewing Republic of Korea troops.

	Republicans	Democrats
President:	Richard M. Nixon	John F. Kennedy
Vice-President:	Henry C. Lodge	Lyndon B. Johnson

Ralph E. Becker Collection

A young and vigorous Richard Nixon is pictured on this 1960 badge, and the continuation of this well-trained politician in office was stressed at the Republican National Convention in Chicago. He took the nomination for president and then chose Henry Cabot Lodge to run with him as vice-president.

Nelson A. Rockefeller, governor of New York, is shown here congratulating the man who defeated him for the Republican nomination. The happy smiles of Mr. and Mrs. Nixon and Rockefeller promised a united front despite their differences.

153

The winning candidates—Nixon and Lodge—with their families were all smiles here as they waved to the crowds of delegates who had nominated them in Chicago. Lodge had served as ambassador to the United Nations and was considered an asset to the party ticket.

As a presidential candidate, Nixon planned to travel many miles to meet the people. An unfortunate accident, where he hurt his knee and had to be hospitalized, changed these plans and weakened his campaign for several weeks.

MEET Mr. & Mrs. RICHARD NIXON

623 ⬛️PⒺ 158

©1960

The theme, "Experience Counts," was repeated wherever Republicans met. However, the Republican civil rights plank did not reflect this experience well enough to suit the South, and Nixon lost many needed black votes because of it.

IF I WERE 21 I'D VOTE FOR NIXON

Ralph E. Becker Collection

Young people were on the march to change the voting age to eighteen, and their voice was beginning to be heard in political circles. This poster shows the support that Nixon received from the youth of the day.

The Republican National Committee issued these fliers to tell the people what the Republican Party had done since 1953. Although the electorate may have read these fliers, the final vote did not reflect belief in Republican policies. Nixon was destined to lose to John Kennedy.

LET'S TELL THE PEOPLE!

Instead of Campaign Talk and Promises The GOP Has Acted!

Many things have been accomplished under Republican policies since 1953, including a whole batch of items the Democrats just talked about for years and years without ever performing, even when they controlled both the White House and both branches of Congress.

Here is a brief checklist of major GOP achievements:

√ Mightiest defense forces in history.
√ Steadiest cost-of-living in recent times.
√ Record number of jobs, with highest pay.
√ First civil rights law in more than 80 years.
√ History's largest highway-building program.
√ The St. Lawrence Seaway, age-old dream, built.
√ Biggest income tax cut in U.S. history.
√ Raised U.S. standard-of-living to highest point yet.
√ Stopped expansion of International communism.
√ Ended Korean War, prevented other conflicts from developing.
√ Gave Atoms-for-Peace program to the world.
√ Put the United States into space exploration, launching 19 earth satellites and space probes.
√ Reversed 20-year trend to centralization of all power in Washington, D.C.
√ Expanded markets for nation's farm products to record heights.
√ Boosted Gross National Production by 35 per cent.
√ Created Small Business Administration, cut Government competition with industry.
√ Achieved Statehood for Hawaii and Alaska.
√ Expanded conservation and resource programs.
√ Bolstered social welfare programs without snuffing out local initiative.
√ Managed the Treasury with prudence, resisting unneeded spending of tax money for special-interest projects.

REPUBLICAN NATIONAL COMMITTEE
1625 Eye Street, N.W., Washington 5, D. C. 102

LET'S TELL THE PEOPLE!

GOP Prudent, Has Record of Being Low-Tax Party

The money the Federal Government spends comes, of course, from the people. The GOP is prudent with the people's money, and this prudence is bitterly opposed by Democrats who propose pumping unneeded billions from the Treasury into various special-interest projects pushed by pressure groups.

— The Battle of the Budget shows the party stands on Federal spending. In Congress in 1959, Democrats voted AGAINST economy on 72 per cent of the roll calls while Republicans pressed for responsible programs.

— Congressional Democrats, attacking balanced GOP budgets, have introduced bills calling for ADDITIONAL Federal spending of more than $325 billion over the next five years.

— When the books are closed on the Eisenhower Administration, four balanced budgets will be recorded—more than Democratic administrations managed in 20 years. Only the pressure of Congressional Democrats and the Democratic Advisory Council stands in the way of a $4.2 billion Federal surplus in the next fiscal year.

— In 1959, Congressional Democrats increased Republican budget requests by a net total of $597 million—and piled on unasked commitments of $11.5 billion which will come due in future years.

— Since Democrats have controlled Congress, the GOP budgets have been increased by a total (through 1959 calendar year) of $5.5 billion.

HISTORY TELLS THE FISCAL STORY:

— The national debt is 91 per cent Democratic. That is, $260 billion of the $290 billion total was incurred when Democrats were in the White House.

— Of the 10 income tax increases since establishment of the tax, ALL BUT ONE have been enacted by Democrats. Of the 9 income tax reductions, 7 were enacted by Republicans—including history's biggest, the 1954 slash which has saved American families $40 billion in the past six years.

REPUBLICAN NATIONAL COMMITTEE
1625 Eye Street, N.W., Washington 5, D. C. 102

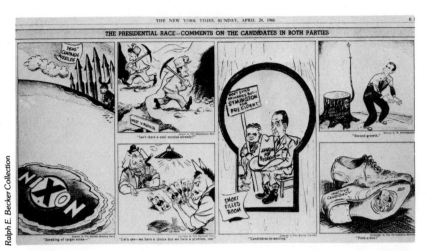

Several outstanding Democrats—such as Humphrey, Johnson, Symington, and Stevenson—were shown on this cartoon. In the Republican camp, only Richard Nixon and Rockefeller were mentioned.

This CORE poster is a forerunner of some of the unhappiest events of the 1960s. CORE was dissatisfied with the progress of civil rights. Nonviolence was not working, and emotions were running high. This became a key issue for both parties as time went on.

John F. Kennedy, shown here campaigning in his private airplane, did not live to serve out his term of office. The entire nation was shocked when an assassin's bullet killed the President in Dallas, Texas, on November 22, 1963. Vice-President Lyndon Johnson was sworn into office at once.

	Republicans	Democrats
President:	Barry M. Goldwater	Lyndon B. Johnson
Vice-President:	William E. Miller	Hubert H. Humphrey

THIS WORLD

GOParty

Prelude to the Cow Palace Overture (Page 5)

San Francisco **Sunday Chronicle** JULY 12, 1964

Once again, the Cow Palace in San Francisco was to host the National Republican Convention in July. Many candidates from all parts of the country were to enter their names in the contest—such names as Rockefeller, Margaret Chase Smith of Maine, Harold Stassen of Minnesota, and of course Barry Goldwater, the senator from Arizona.

REPUBLICANS CONVENE IN SAN FRANCISCO
JULY 13

A problem as old as the two-party system will challenge Republicans as they meet July 13 in San Francisco. From a string of attractive candidates, they must pick one man strong enough to unseat a President eyeing the White House for a second term. Will he be selected from among the GOP hopefuls whose names make news every day? Or will a "dark horse" finally get the nomination?

The delegates will listen to the arguments of all contenders and then make their decision in the Cow Palace, a 30,000 square-foot arena for some of the nation's largest conventions, exhibitions, and livestock shows. Built during the depression, the huge structure earned its name from a disgruntled newspaper correspondent who complained that "while people are being evicted from their homes, a palace is being built for cows."

The main hall has a seating capacity of 16,000. It is flanked by two 49,000 square-foot halls, available for use by the press and television networks. Two nearby exhibit buildings, with a combined floor space of 120,000 square feet, will house private offices and press and committee rooms. More than 5,000 automobiles can be fitted into the parking areas, and over 5,000 persons each hour can be served in the various restaurants and food stands.

The 700-room Fairmont Hotel on Nob Hill will be convention headquarters. A small community in itself, it often serves 8,000 meals daily. Its 20 different banquet rooms can accommodate from 25 to 1,900 guests.

The Golden Gate City, with its temperate year-round climate, is one of the most picturesque in the nation. Some of its many restaurants, night clubs, and cafes are known around the world. To these attractive facilities, San Francisco adds the value of experience in playing host to America's biggest political shows. The Democrats met here in 1920, the Republicans in 1956.

3

It was at the Cow Palace that the Republican Platform came out against the expansion of federal powers and for an end to diplomatic relations with Iron Curtain countries. The platform promised full implementation of the Civil Rights Act of 1964, with a qualified declaration against discrimination.

CAPITOL HILL CLUB News

Volume XV, Number 8   Published Monthly on Capitol Hill   August, 1964

Of the eight candidates nominated at the Republican Convention, only Barry Goldwater made a big splash, with 883 votes on the first ballot. The nomination was then made unanimous. For vice-president, the convention chose Congressman William Miller of New York, shown here with Barry Goldwater as they accepted the cheers of the delegates.

GO WITH GOLDWATER

Words by
TOM McDONNELL

Music by
OTIS CLEMENTS

$1.00

THE VINCENT YOUMANS CO., INC.
157 WEST 57th STREET · NEW YORK 19, N.Y.

"Go with Goldwater" may have been the slogan put on sheet music, but morality in government was a repeated theme in Goldwater speeches. This emphasis on morality was caused by certain political scandals surrounding some of the Democrats in government at that time.

This Goldwater handkerchief may have been waved on behalf of the Republicans or worn proudly by its Republican owner. Those people who supported the candidate did so with great enthusiasm and determination.

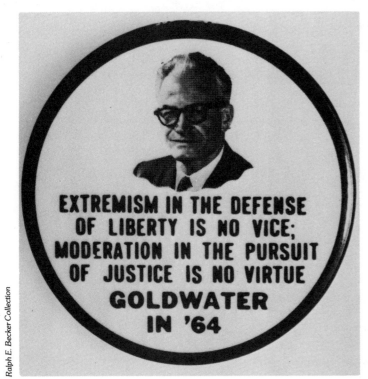

The slogan written on this political button was to counteract Democratic charges of "extremism" for the Republican candidate. Barry Goldwater was indeed conservative in his outlook at this time.

Campaign buttons showed some of the women behind the men: Eleanor Roosevelt, Edith Willkie, Mamie Eisenhower, Pat Nixon, Lady Bird Johnson, and Margaret Chase Smith. While these were not all Republican women, they all had impact on their party as well as the country.

Margaret Chase Smith, Senator from Maine, is shown here at a rally to draft her for president. Although her standing as a woman senator was impressive, she could not command enough delegates to carry the Republican Party.

Differences in the Republican Party on issues could not be healed sufficiently by November 3. The lack of strong support for Barry Goldwater returned Johnson to the White House with Humphrey serving as his vice-president.

	Republicans	Democrats
President:	**Richard M. Nixon**	Hubert H. Humphrey
Vice-President:	**Spiro T. Agnew**	Edmund S. Muskie

Ralph E. Becker Collection

Nineteen hundred and sixty-eight was a year of many candidates for both major parties. Democratic Senator McCarthy of Minnesota put his name up as an anti-Vietnam War candidate and entered several primaries. Although he campaigned vigorously, he did not ultimately win the nomination from his party.

Dick Gregory actively campaigned and was well received by the black voters. Despite this and his frequent requests for a write-in vote on his behalf, his candidacy accomplished very little.

163

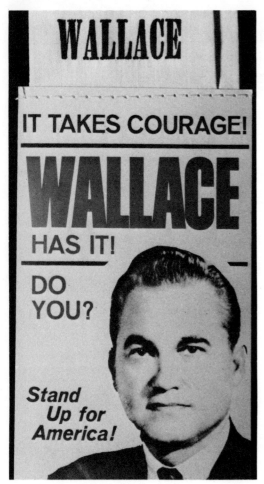

Governor George Wallace of Alabama represented his own minor party—the American Independent Party—with his stand against black integration. He drew support from John Birchers and others who were radically inclined on the racial issues.

The war in Vietnam was a major issue in this campaign. President Johnson announced the cessation of bombing raids on North Vietnam at the same time he said he would not run again. The Republicans came out for a settlement of the Vietnam War in rather broad terms in the Party platform of 1968.

Ralph E. Becker Collection

Once again, Richard M. Nixon came to the front as a presidential candidate for the Republican Party. He began actively campaigning in the primary elections around the country and went to Miami Beach, Florida, in August with a great deal of confidence that he would win the nomination.

Although twelve candidates names were presented to the Republican National Party at the convention, Richard Nixon won the nomination on the first ballot. He chose Governor Spiro T. Agnew of Maryland for his running mate.

Convention Memory Lingers on – as the Winners Hit Campaign Trail

This picture of the Willard Hotel in Washington, D.C., shows the two Republican candidates. According to the party platform adopted in Miami, Nixon and Agnew stood for a solution to the "crisis of the cities," for law and order, and for a settlement of the Vietnam War in very broad terms.

The campaign waged by Nixon and Agnew was basically a "law and order" campaign. In a country troubled by racial discontent and rioting, this had a popular appeal to the average middle-class citizen.

It was the elephant that was destined to go to the White House in 1968. The bank shown here bore the names of the next president and vice-president of the United States.

Senator Hubert Humphrey of Minnesota was the Democratic nominee for president and Senator Muskie of Maine ran for vice-president. This donkey bank was a popular campaign item at that time.

The Poor People's Campaign for civil rights and racial equality was often seen in Washington during the tumultuous 1960s. Although the Republicans did give some lip service to its causes, the Republican attitudes were more geared to the middle-class American.

1972

President:
Vice-President:

Republicans
Richard M. Nixon
Spiro T. Agnew

Democrats
George McGovern
R. Sargent Shriver

In June 1971, President Nixon signed into law the twenty-sixth amendment of the Constitution, which gave eighteen-, nineteen-, and twenty-year olds the right to vote. The signing took place at the White House with many young people looking on.

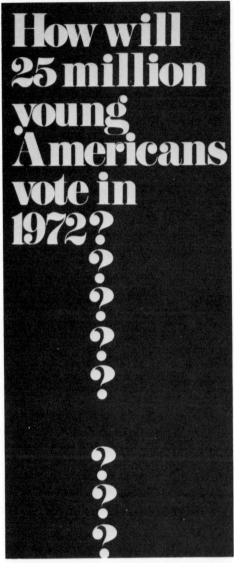

How will 25 million young Americans vote in 1972?
?
?
?
?
?
?
?
?
?

The youth vote became a prominent issue in the campaign of 1972. The question asked in this poster was one that all politicians were concerned with.

The tennis shoes pictured here with the word "vote" on both the soles and the canvas part of the shoe were symbols of the new young voters who would vote for the first time in this election.

¡Hermanos y Hermanas
REGISTRESE
Para Votar Hoy Mismo!

El Lugar

La Fecha

Brothers and Sisters
REGISTER
To Vote Today!

Place

Date

YCF youth citizenship fund, inc.   2317 M Street, N.W., Washington, D.C. 20037

Youth appeal posters such as this one were put out by the Youth Citizenship Fund. The young people hoped to make a showing for the candidate of their choice.

Jewelry was designed to appeal to the new young voters and was frequently seen on college campuses throughout the country.

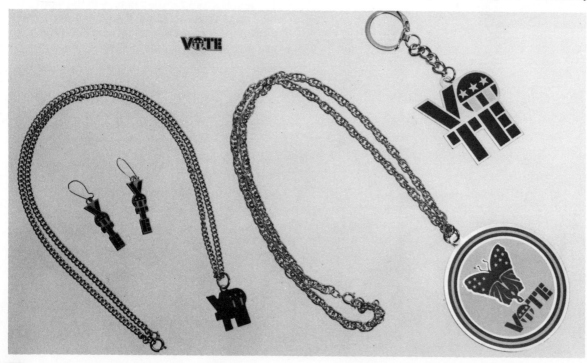

The lettering on this poster reads—"In 1776, voting was a revolutionary idea . . . It still is." The young man playing the flute in the picture is a young voter, 1972 variety.

Vietnam was the major foreign policy issue of the day. The Republican platform promised that the administration would not abandon the South Vietnamese. A gradual phasing-out was to be the continued American policy.

This collection of campaign buttons shows those both for and against Richard Nixon. (The impeachment button shown here was not around in 1972. The story of impeachment was to come later on.)

Unrest surrounding the Republicans came from more sources than just the Vietnam War. Vice President Agnew was not making many friends with his outspoken words such as "effete snob." The badge shown here was pro-Republican—it picked up the unfortunate remark and turned it into a support of peace.

The Republican National Convention was held in Miami Beach, Florida, and Richard Nixon was nominated again. This patriotic sheet music declares, "Richard Nixon is the one."

Fans such as this one may have been waved by Republican delegates to keep cool, as well as to keep the peace and prosperity of the country. This picture of Richard Nixon may have been taken several years before when he was a younger but still eager politician.

Many Republicans wore this political button as they listened to Nixon's acceptance speech. This speech included a review of his past four years in office and a promise to continue on for still another term.

This Nixon-Agnew plate showed the solidarity of the two candidates. Despite rumors of political problems in Maryland involving Agnew, Nixon stood behind his vice-president.

In the early 1970s, this banner was drawn and used in both peace and impeachment of President Nixon demonstrations. This active group fought long and hard for changes in both domestic and foreign policies.

The fight for full women's rights dates back to the nineteenth century but continued in the twentieth. This first national political caucus took place in February 1973 in Houston, Texas, at the Rice Hotel. The women shown left to right are Gwen Cheny, Betty Friedan, Patricia Schroeder, and Liz Carpenter.

Problems faced the Republican Party after the election of 1972—not the least of which was Spiro T. Agnew. Mr. Agnew was forced to resign from the vice-presidency on October 10, 1973, to face charges of political corruption in his own state of Maryland.

Corruption in politics is not unusual but the break-in of Democratic headquarters in 1973 and the ensuing cover-up of that break-in had repercussions that were felt in the White House. The Republican Party and the nation were faced with the possible impeachment of President Nixon.

A shocked country watched television broadcasts of the trial of the Watergate criminals. Here, Judge Sirica is shown listening to damning tapes in the courtroom. Because of these tapes, President Nixon was forced to resign from office on August 9, 1974. Gerald R. Ford, the appointed vice-president who had replaced Agnew, became president of the United States. This drawing of the courtroom scene was by Freda Reiter.

	Republicans	Democrats
President:	Gerald R. Ford	**Jimmy Carter**
Vice-President:	Robert Dole	**Walter Mondale**

The Republican National Convention met in Kansas City, Missouri, in August, at which time trays like this one were sold as mementos. Even with air conditioning the tempers were to flare at this convention before the nominations were made final.

Bandannas showing the Republican elephant overcoming the donkey were used to create enthusiasm at the convention.

The elephant was sure to crush the peanut if Jerry Ford was the candidate for president. Ford had a clean bill of health on the Watergate problems, a sound and stable personality, and was generally a popular man. Had Ford won the election, he would have gone back to the White House as an elected servant of the people for the first time.

The same Republican elephant was going to crush the peanut, but the candidate's name this time was Ronald Reagan, governor of California. Reagan had many supporters in Kansas City, but not quite enough.

ROCKY: DON'T STEAL my sign!

Nelson Rockefeller, governor of New York, was also a presidential possibility at Kansas City. This anti-Rockefeller poster was waved the night after Rockefeller tore up a sign for Reagan.

A WOMAN'S PLACE IS IN THE HOUSE AND IN THE SENATE

This banner was made by the Equal Rights Amendment forces and showed up at both major party conventions in 1976. The women were working toward full equality and made themselves well known all over the country.

President Ford '76

The President Ford Committee, Howard H. Calloway, Chairman, Robert C. Moot, Treasurer.

Gerald Ford won the nomination to carry the Republican banner to the White House. The vice-presidential candidate was Robert Dole, senator from Kansas.

Campaign objects ranged from derby hats to inflated elephants, and most of them were made up quickly with both Ford's and Dole's names on them. The delegates left the convention ready to fight what turned out to be a losing battle.

Robert Dole of Kansas was to spend many miles on the campaign trail. Here he is shown with President Ford preparing to make his acceptance speech.

President Ford is shown shaking hands with Democratic candidate Jimmy Carter and Mrs. Carter after a television debate. Through television, the country grew to know both candidates well.

The vice-presidential candidates also used the medium of television to hold debates. A smiling Mr. Mondale on the left faces a smiling Robert Dole.

This large collection of presidential campaign buttons includes most of the candidates for 1976. A tremendous amount of history can be told from the names on these buttons.

Despite strenuous campaigning, Republican President Ford was not to return to the White House in 1976. Jimmy Carter, the peanut farmer from Georgia, won the election.

Bibliography

Binkley, Wilfred E. *American Political Parties*. New York: Alfred A. Knopf, 1963.

Brogan, D.W. *Politics in America*. New York: Harper and Brothers, 1954.

Buchanan, Lamont. *Ballot for Americans*. New York: E. P. Dutton, 1956.

Chambers, William Nisbet and Burnham, Walter Dean. *The American Party Systems*. New York: Oxford University Press, 1975.

Clements, John. *Chronology of the United States*. McGraw Hill, Inc., 1975.

Congressional Quarterly, Inc. *Elections '76*. Washington, D.C.: Congressional Quarterly, 1976.

Congressional Quarterly, Inc. *National Party Conventions 1831-1972*. Washington, D.C.: Congressional Quarterly, 1976.

Durant, John and Alice. *Pictorial History of American Presidents*. A. S. Barnes & Co., 1955.

Felknor, Bruce L. *Dirty Politics*. New York: W. W. Norton & Company, Inc., 1966.

Goodman, William. *The Two-Party System in the United States*. New York: D. Van Nostrand Company, Inc., 1964.

Harsch, Joseph C. *The Role of Political Parties U.S.A.* Washington, D.C.: League of Women Voters Education Fund, 1955.

Hess, Stephen and Kaplan, Milton. *The Ungentlemanly Art*. New York: Macmillan Publishing Co., 1975.

Hoff, Syd. *Editorial and Political Cartooning*. New York: Stravon Educational Press, 1976.

Hofstadter, Richard, Miller, William and Aaron, Daniel. *The United States, The History of a Republic*. New Jersey: Prentice-Hall, Inc., 1967.

Kahler, James G. *Hail to the Chief*. Princeton: Pyne Press, 1972.

Kane, Joseph Nathan. *Facts About the Presidents*. New York: H. W. Wilson Company, 1974.

Murphy, Paul L. *Political Parties in American History*. Vol. 3. New York: G. P. Putnam Sons, 1974.

Porter, Kirk H. and Johnson, Donald Bruce. *National Party Platforms 1840-1964*. Urbana and London: University of Illinois Press, 1966.

Roseboom, Eugene H. *A History of Presidential Elections*. New York: Macmillan Company, 1970.

Schnapper, M.B. *Grand Old Party*. Washington, D.C.: Public Affairs Press, 1955.

Silber, Irwin. *Songs America Voted By*. Pennsylvania: Stackpole Books, 1971.

Taylor, Tim. *The Book of Presidents*. New York: Arno Press. 1972.

Vinson, J. Chal. *Thomas Nast, Political Cartoonist*. Athens, Georgia: University of Georgia Press, 1967.

Williams, T. Harry, Current, Richard M. and Friedel, Frank. *History of the United States Since 1865*. New York: Alfred A. Knopf, 1961.

Index

D4